MW01626947

Jack Skeen | Greg Miller | Aaron Hill

THE INDEPENDENCE WORKBOOK

Part of the Circle Blueprint System

Published by:
Griffin Publishing
314 E. Lake Shore Drive
Tower Lakes, IL 60010
Phone: (847) 910-1640

ISBN: 978-0-9993388-1-0

Library of Congress Control Number: 2017956814

Printed in the United States of America

TABLE OF CONTENTS

INTRODUCTION TO INDEPENDENCE

INTRODUCTION TO INDEPENDENCE

The Independence Workbook offers a system to help you decode the conscious and unconscious factors that affect your success. Independence is the first of four fundamental development areas of *The Circle Blueprint*—which you may have read, but which is not entirely essential. There are also workbooks for the other three fundamental development areas (Power, Humility, and Purpose), and you may wish to also work through the other three after you work through the Independence Workbook to more fully develop your Circle Blueprint. The system in this workbook is intended for anyone with an interest in developing a higher mastery of the element of Independence. People who develop a mastery of Independence have a clear understanding of who they are and are not concerned with giving way to pleasure others at the expense of that sense of self—they take full responsibility for their life and live free of self-doubt, comparison, and insecurity.

ASSESSING YOUR INDEPENDENCE

If you have read *The Circle Blueprint*, you are likely familiar with the self-assessment tool available at www.thecircleblueprint.com. This tool, which we will explain below for those who are either unfamiliar or who want a reminder, helps you understand where you are on various factors that constitute the element of Independence. If you are comfortable with the assessment process, you may want to proceed to the After Self-Assessment section.

SIX FACTORS AFFECT OUR ABILITY TO GAIN INDEPENDENCE:

1. **Crisis Prone:** Creating situations that either do not have to exist, or that do not actually exist in reality.
2. **Autonomous:** Living free of comparison and relying healthily on self and others.
3. **Pleasing:** Adapting to the real or perceived needs of others in unhealthy ways.
4. **Pretentious:** Needing to appear in a light more favorable than one actually is.

5. **Personal Commitment:** Having goals, operationalizing them into actionable plans, and disciplining yourself to execute those plans.
6. **Reliance:** Being controlled by someone or something else.

The Circle Blueprint provides in-depth explanations of these factors, but this overview should give you the gist of it, and the results of your assessment, or even honest self-reflection on these issues, will let you know where you may need further development or better balance.

Specifically, the assessment results provide descriptions on our "Thriving Scale." On each factor, you should have a score.

1. I am ***hanging on*** by my fingernails. Despite all I have accomplished, my life isn't good at all.
2. I am ***eroding***. I'm not desperate, but my life is a grind and does not seem to be headed in a positive direction.
3. I am ***treading water*** and just sort of enduring my situation. My life isn't bad, but I would not say it is good, either.
4. I am ***growing***. My life is on a positive trajectory. Certainly, it could be better, but I am reasonably satisfied and optimistic about the future.
5. I am ***thriving***. I am creatively engaged in my work and life. I am at the top of my game. I feel energized, balanced, healthy, and happy.

AFTER SELF-ASSESSMENT

Once you have an idea of where you are on each factor, you can proceed to the exercise series. We have broken these out according to where you fall on the Thriving Scale. In this way, you can go through various exercises according to where you are. That is, if you are hanging on, complete the exercises that align with hanging on, and if you are growing, you can complete the exercises that align with growing. There are no exercises for areas where you are thriving because you do not need further development in those factors. We have included multiple sessions to allow you to work on developing each factor over time. After you complete Session 1, you can move to Session 2 and so on. Further, you can also repeat the assessment or even work on your own development over time—after you complete the “treading water” exercises, for example, you can move onto the “growing” exercises. We have often found it helpful to revisit the exercises at one level of the Thriving Scale a few times if need be, and in other instances, just moving to the next level after one pass may be sufficient. The system is flexible for you and 100 percent self-driven—you complete the exercise series as you see fit, but this offers you a system for developing your Circle Blueprint at your own pace and in total privacy.

EXERCISE SERIES:
CRISIS PRONE

FACTOR – CRISIS PRONE

This construct describes the traits of people who tend to fill their lives with drama. They prefer to be emotionally upset. They may have a pattern of procrastination, waiting for the pressure of deadlines to motivate them to action. On the other hand, those who are not crisis prone have control over their emotional reactions. They are more thoughtful and organized. They are much better able to plan and to stick with their plan than are those who are easily distracted by their emotional distress, much of which, as we will see, is of their own creation.

SELF-ASSESSED RATING - HANGING ON

You are constantly in crisis and have no stable foundation on which to build your life.

SESSION 1

EXERCISE 1A – CRISIS PRONE, HANGING ON

You are drowning in drama. The emotional upset you create so dominates your life that it is in serious trouble. Remember that drama is a way of seeing the world around you in a way that creates so much turmoil that it completely distracts you from productive thoughts and activity. Now is the time for you to make an assessment of your life. What is drama costing you?

TASK: Make a list of the price you are paying for feeling helpless, angry, resentful, embittered, judgmental, and hopeless. Review this list every day for the next week and add to it everything that comes to mind.

EXERCISE 2A – CRISIS PRONE, HANGING ON

Now that you realize that you must turn your life around, it is time to identify the drama that surrounds you. There are two parts. The first is the drama others invite you into. The second is the drama you create with your thoughts, words, and actions.

TASK: Make a list of all of the situations you encounter that are characterized by negativity, complaining, judging, blaming, arguing, gossiping, justifying, and worrying. Then add to it all of the ways you create unnecessary upset in your life. This might be a very long list and may seem to describe almost everything you do and everywhere you go. That is okay. Review your list every day for one week and add to it.

EXERCISE 3A – CRISIS PRONE, HANGING ON

It is time to begin to create some order in the drama that overwhelms your life. Remember that the drama is not your life, even if it seems to take up almost all of your time and attention. Your life is a place of calm. It is a place of strength.

TASK: Take your list of drama and prioritize it from the most important to the least important. The most important drama is the one you most urgently need to resolve in order to begin to recover your life. It is the biggest obstacle you face. Revisit your list every day for the next week and reorder your list of drama until it looks accurate.

EXERCISE 4A – CRISIS PRONE, HANGING ON

Imagine your life without this most important drama. How would you feel? What would be better? Can you envision some measure of control over your circumstances as if someone threw you a line when you were drowning? Now you can hope. Now you have a way to make things better. You have taken a first step toward reversing the pattern of your life. Real change happens only after you can imagine it. This is your opportunity to begin regaining control of your life.

TASK: Take a few minutes and write a description of how much better your life will be when you are free from this one drama. Reread this every day for the next week and take a few minutes to enjoy the freedom you will have created for yourself.

SESSION 2

EXERCISE 1B – CRISIS PRONE, HANGING ON

Perhaps the most common type of drama for those who are hanging on by their fingernails is victim drama. When you are engaged in victim drama, you feel at the mercy of life. Your life is filled with worry and anxiety. You imagine all the ways your life is going wrong and feel helpless to turn it around. Here is your opportunity to come to see how you show up as a victim in your life.

TASK: List every circumstance in which you feel helpless. List every relationship where you pretend to be who you aren't in order to get by. List every worry and concern you have about your life. I know this might take some time. Take time every day for the next week to add to your list.

EXERCISE 2B – CRISIS PRONE, HANGING ON

In order for you to maintain victim drama, you must have other people in either the villain or the hero role in your life. You make people villains when you see them as the cause of your problems. You make people heroes when you expect them to protect, provide for, or understand you as a victim. Not only will you see people through these lenses, you will create people treating you in one of those two ways. People who care for you may grow impatient with your unwillingness to take responsibility for your life and so will eventually become judgmental and frustrated. You will have turned them into villains. Others will continue to cut you slack and make excuses for you, even when it isn't best for you. They will become your heroes.

TASK: Go through your list of victim drama and write down who is playing either the villain or hero roles in each drama. Review the list every day for the next week and add names.

EXERCISE 3B – CRISIS PRONE, HANGING ON

In order for you to release yourself from being dominated by villain drama, you must learn to face your fears and push through them. Allowing your life to be dominated by fear undermines your ability to create anything good for yourself.

Do you remember being chased as a child? The fear of being caught makes you run as fast as you can. But, no matter how fast you run, the fear only gets bigger. It is only when you stop running and turn around to face your fear that you have any chance of making something good happen. Pick one villain from your list. It might be wise to choose the one you fear the least. Small victories can provide courage to take on bigger challenges. What do you need to say or do to free yourself from your fear of this person and what they might do? Write it down. You might be terrified to even consider taking a stand because you are so used to being dominated by your life.

TASK: Think through how you will say or do what you have to say or do. Now, go do it.

EXERCISE 4B – CRISIS PRONE, HANGING ON

Since you are hanging on by your fingernails, your life must be in disarray. You have not taken care of yourself very well. And, while you may have had numerous people become frustrated and judgmental toward you, it is likely that you have also either found or trained others who take care of you even in areas where you could take care of yourself. You have become skilled at enticing people to rescue you so you can avoid facing necessary challenges. Now, it is time to take back the responsibility to do for yourself what you have been unwilling to do.

TASK: Your first task is to list every responsibility you should and could do for yourself that you are allowing others to do for you. Then write next to each one how you would take on that task. Finally, go to each person on whom you have been depending, thank them for their help, and tell them it is no longer needed. Take the next week to execute this exercise.

SESSION 3

EXERCISE 1C – CRISIS PRONE, HANGING ON

The second type of drama for those who are hanging on by their fingernails is villain drama. When you are engaged in villain drama, you fill your life with judgments and criticism about others. Instead of focusing on ways you can regain control of your life, you spend almost all of your time being angry and critical toward others. You may not even notice that your anger toward others does nothing to improve your situation. But, it may distract you from attending to your circumstances and give you an excuse not to act. Here is your opportunity to come to see how you show up as a villain in your life.

TASK: List everyone you criticize and judge. This might be a long list. I know this might take some time. Take time every day for the next week to add to your list.

EXERCISE 2C – CRISIS PRONE, HANGING ON

In order for you to maintain villain drama, you must have other people in either the victim or the hero role in your life. You make people victims when you dominate them with your anger, frustration, and complaints and make them fearful of telling you when they have had enough. You make people heroes when you expect them to understand, make excuses, and put up with your ugly attitudes and words. Not only will you see people through these lenses, you will create people treating you in one of those two ways. People who care for you will gradually conform to the pressure of your anger and cower in your presence. You will have turned them into victims. Others will continue to cut you slack and make excuses for you, even when it isn't best for you. They will become your heroes.

TASK: Go through your list of villain drama and write down who is playing either the victim or hero roles in each drama. Review the list every day for the next week and add names.

EXERCISE 3C – CRISIS PRONE, HANGING ON

In order for you to release yourself from being dominated by villain drama, you must learn to shift your focus from what is wrong with others to what is wrong with your life. Allowing your life to be dominated by anger and judgment undermines your ability to focus on creating anything good for yourself. Do you remember the schoolyard bully? While he may have thought he had power, everyone secretly resented him. His social circle was maintained only through intimidation.

TASK: Make a list of the people you are bullying with your anger and frustration. Who is walking carefully when they are around you? Who is unwilling to tell you how they truly feel? Notice who seems timid in your company. Practice with one person on your list. Be quiet and listen to them. Be careful not to become frustrated or judgmental. Focus on creating the space for them to show up more fully. Practice with this person every day this week. See if you like what you are creating for yourself.

EXERCISE 4C – CRISIS PRONE, HANGING ON

Since you are hanging on by your fingernails, your life must be in disarray. You have not taken care of yourself very well. And, while numerous people may have been fearful of you, it is likely that you have also either found or trained others who put up with your bullying self by excusing it away or minimizing the damage it does to others and to you. You have become skilled at enticing people to rescue you so you can avoid facing necessary challenges. Now, it is time to take back the responsibility to do for yourself what you have been unwilling to do.

TASK: Your first task is to shift your judgments from others to yourself. How is your life a mess? How did you let it get this way? What are you going to do about it? Next, write next to each one how you would take on that task. Make one change each day this week.

SESSION 4

EXERCISE 1D – CRISIS PRONE, HANGING ON

Since you are hanging on by your fingernails, it is unlikely that you have a great deal of hero drama in your life. Nevertheless, it is worthwhile to search for any and to free yourself from its grip. Hero drama shows up when you don't hold others accountable to be their very best self. You may actually make an unconscious agreement with people in your life that you won't hold them accountable to have a functional life if they don't hold you accountable for the same. In this way, you remain codependent in having dysfunctional lives.

TASK: Spend the next 20 minutes considering who you might not be holding fully accountable. It is especially smart to consider spouses, children, and coworkers for your list. Revisit your list every day to add more names.

EXERCISE 2D – CRISIS PRONE, HANGING ON

For everyone for whom you are being a hero, you are making them a victim or villain. They are victims if you make it okay for them to not take responsibility for cultivating healthy lives. You might support them in having bad habits or not push them to dream bigger dreams. They are villains if they are doing things that get in their way and limit their effectiveness and you aren't calling them out.

TASK: Make a list of all of the important people in your life who you are allowing to be victims or villains in their own life drama. Review the list each day and add names.

EXERCISE 3D – CRISIS PRONE, HANGING ON

Review your list of victims. These are the people in your life who you allow to believe that they are not strong enough to solve their own problems and to build a wonderful life. Your sympathy undermines their strength. It may not be easy when your own life is in disarray to take the excuses away from others for their problems, but it is the very best thing you can do in their lives to do so.

TASK: Withdraw sympathy from each person on your list. Meet with each person this week. Tell them that you have been letting them off the hook for an aspect of their lives and you won't do that any longer. Show up in a more powerful way, encouraging them to face their problems and challenges squarely and honestly.

EXERCISE 4D – CRISIS PRONE, HANGING ON

Review your list of villains. These are the people who are actively doing things that get in their way. They are bullying others, living their lives complaining about others, gossiping, slandering, and being negative, and you have been excusing it away. If you are honest, you can clearly see that their drama makes it difficult for anyone to want to be around them. They are severely limiting the effectiveness of their lives. They need to face the consequences of their choices without being rescued.

TASK: Go to each person on your list and tell them that you have been covering for them and that you won't do this any longer. Explain that you believe in them too much to excuse away their poor choices.

FACTOR – CRISIS PRONE

This construct describes the traits of people who tend to fill their lives with drama. They prefer to be emotionally upset. They may have a pattern of procrastination, waiting for the pressure of deadlines to motivate them to action. On the other hand, those who are not crisis prone have control over their emotional reactions. They are more thoughtful and organized. They are much better able to plan and to stick with their plan than are those who are easily distracted by their emotional distress, much of which, as we will see, is of their own creation.

SELF-ASSESSED RATING - ERODING

You are often in crisis, and the foundation for your life is rarely adequate to create stability.

SESSION 1

EXERCISE 1A – CRISIS PRONE, ERODING

Your life is eroding because the drama in your life is greater than your ability to resist or overcome it. You are caught in conflicts, resentments, and/or frustrations that distract you from making healthy choices. As a result, your life is becoming weaker instead of stronger. It is time for you to face the way you are living.

TASK: List the cost you are paying for living in drama. You may have financial issues, health issues, emotional issues, or bad habits that are directly the result of unresolved drama. Spend time every day for the next week adding to your list.

EXERCISE 2A – CRISIS PRONE, ERODING

Now that you realize that your life is diminishing largely because of the drama in it, it is time for you to assess the sources of drama. Remember that drama is defined as unnecessary emotional upset. It is anything and everything that distracts you from seeing life more realistically and taking responsibility for your own well-being. It includes feeling at the mercy of other people or life circumstances. It includes worry about things that are out of your control. It includes resentments and guilt about things that happened in the past. It includes holding grudges and unresolved conflict.

TASK: Make a list of all of the drama currently in your life. Revisit that list every day for one week and add to it whatever comes to mind.

EXERCISE 3A - CRISIS PRONE, ERODING

Now that you have your list of drama, prioritize it from the most important issue to the least. You may notice that one item on your list catches your attention because it seems like the source of all of the others. If you only resolved this issue, your life would stop eroding. It could be a bad marriage that you have avoided addressing because you fear the consequences of divorce. Or, you may have a secret that has been creating guilt. Whatever the issue, you know you need to face it or you will continue to get weaker. This should be at the top of your list.

TASK: Review your list every day for the next week and reorder the items until it feels right to you.

EXERCISE 4A – CRISIS PRONE, ERODING

You have identified the most important source of drama for you to resolve. Now, envision how much better your life will be when it is behind you. This is an important exercise because envisioning the future is a critical step in change. Until you can clearly see what you want, it is very difficult to create it.

TASK: Make a list of the benefits you will get from eliminating this drama from your life. This may be the very anchor that is pulling your life under water. Reread your list every day and allow yourself to enjoy the idea of your new strength and freedom.

SESSION 2

EXERCISE 1B – CRISIS PRONE, ERODING

Most people who are eroding tend to have a fair amount of victim drama in their lives. You are stuck in victim drama if you find yourself feeling out of control of your life, are dominated by others, have surrendered your self-determination, and are filled with worries and concerns that limit your ability to cope.

TASK: In order for you to become more aware of where you are playing the victim role, list every circumstance and relationship where you are involved in victim energy. Write one example for each. Review your list each day for the next week and add illustrations.

EXERCISE 2B – CRISIS PRONE, ERODING

Your victim drama is only maintained by seeing (and creating) others as villains and heroes in your life. Perhaps the oppression you think is coming from others and is the reason you are eroding is truly the result of your creating villains by playing the victim role. People who used to genuinely support you may have grown tired of hearing your excuses and have become demanding because they have run out of patience. Others may keep making excuses for you and have been willing to support your lack of accountability for your life for too long.

TASK: Next to each drama on your list, name the people you see as villains and heroes. Review your list every day for the next week and add names.

EXERCISE 3B – CRISIS PRONE, ERODING

You know you have allowed your life to fall into disrepair because you have been too afraid to take on your responsibility for your own life. You have blamed others for holding you back or for overwhelming you with their demands and judgments. But this is an excuse. It is time for you to take back your independence by standing up to those you have feared. You may believe you need their support but you are selling yourself short.

TASK: Take one of the people you have placed in the villain role and write what you would have to say or do to end the drama. Practice saying it until you are comfortable. Now, have the conversation.

EXERCISE 4B – CRISIS PRONE, ERODING

You have been allowing many people to take on responsibilities for you that you should be doing for yourself. It is because of this that your life has gradually become weaker. You are making yourself excessively dependent on those whom you have shaped into your heroes. It is time for you to retake your responsibility for your life.

TASK: Make a list of those things for which you need to retake responsibility and do so. Thank each person on whom you have been depending and tell them their assistance is no longer required.

SESSION 3

EXERCISE 1C – CRISIS PRONE, ERODING

Most people who are eroding tend to have a fair amount of villain drama in their lives. You are stuck in villain drama if you find your anger, judgments, and domination of others is eroding the quality of your life.

TASK: In order for you to become more aware of where you are playing the villain role, list the number of healthy relationships you lost over your lifetime because you were simply too disagreeable for people to tolerate. Each of these is a potential ally in building a stronger and better life. Driving them away has contributed to your life eroding. You have been too difficult to keep a job, too negative for anyone to want to live with you. Revisit your list each day this week and add names and opportunities you have lost by playing the villain role.

EXERCISE 2C – CRISIS PRONE, ERODING

Your villain drama is only maintained by seeing (and creating) others as victims and heroes in your life. By bullying people into submission, you can create the appearance of support, but in doing so you have surrounded yourself with victims you have created. You may also be able to find some (though few) heroes who will blame your hostility, anger, and judgments on your childhood or make some other excuse. In truth, people find you difficult to be around and don't enjoy your company.

TASK: Next to each drama on your list, name the people you see as villains and heroes. Review your list every day for the next week and add names.

EXERCISE 3C – CRISIS PRONE, ERODING

You know you have bullied some people into pretending to support you because they fear inciting your anger. You have been demanding and overbearing, insisting on your own way to the point where you don't leave much room for others to be themselves in your company. Wherever you go people become victims of your negative energy. You have undermined your ability to have a positive and successful life by having so much villain drama. Now it is time to let it go. You can do so by making room in your life for people to show up however they are. It is not for you to judge them but to learn from them. Let them teach you how you can build your life to be better and stronger.

TASK: Pick one person on your list of those you have made victims in your life and commit to being kind and gracious to them. Spend time with this person every day over the next week and transform the relationship by bringing positive energy and by listening attentively.

EXERCISE 4C – CRISIS PRONE, ERODING

Your life is eroding largely because you have been more occupied with drama than you have been focused on making constructive choices. In addition to bullying people into submission, you likely have attracted a number of people who know you are difficult but they make excuses for the way you behave or cover for you because they feel sorry for you. These are your heroes. The problem is that they would serve you better if they allowed you to experience the full consequences of your negative energy and if they held you accountable for the messes you make. It is your job to end the drama by taking full responsibility for the outcome of how you are choosing to show up in the world around you.

TASK: Using your list of heroes, write next to each how they are protecting you or excusing your behavior. Use this list to begin taking over responsibility for each item on the list. Revisit your list every day this week and take on a new task each day.

SESSION 4

EXERCISE 1D – CRISIS PRONE, ERODING

Most people who are eroding tend to have little hero drama in their lives. They are more prone to be villains and victims. You are stuck in hero drama to the extent you excuse and overlook your lack of responsibility for the welfare of your own life by surrounding yourself with others whose lives are in poor shape. You may not only gravitate toward friendships and partnerships with dysfunctional people, but you may also encourage lack of effort and responsibility on the part of important people in your life.

TASK: In order for you to become more aware of where you are playing the hero role, list the key relationships in your life (partner, children, coworkers, and friends). Who are you allowing to be less than they could be? For them, you are playing the hero. Revisit this list every day for the next week and add names.

EXERCISE 2D – CRISIS PRONE, ERODING

You are stuck in hero drama when you encourage the people in your life to be less than they can be because it makes you feel better about the lack of power and strength in your own life. As a hero, you will invite people to be either victims or villains.

TASK: Review your list from your last exercise. Ask yourself two questions: *First, do I invite anyone on this list to be dependent on me such that they don't have to face challenges and opportunities in their lives?* If so, they are your victims. *Second, do I put up with and make excuses for people in my life who have bad interpersonal habits and so get in the way of their own success?* If so, these are your villains. Revisit your list each day this week and add names and insights.

EXERCISE 3D – CRISIS PRONE, ERODING

Review your list of victims. Next to each name list how you are supporting them in avoiding taking on challenges that would strengthen their lives. What is the next step for them to take on their journey? What do they need to take on that they are avoiding? How could you encourage them to move forward and withdraw your acceptance of the status quo in their lives without wounding the relationship?

TASK: Take one person on your list and talk to them about their next step. Notice how it feels to support their growth.

EXERCISE 4D – CRISIS PRONE, ERODING

Review your list of villains. These are the people whom you see getting in their own way and don't do anything to help them. You are unwilling to confront them because you don't want others to confront you for your own bad behavior. Make a list of the things you see each person doing that they need to give up. They might not be controlling their temper. They might be drinking too much. They might be abusive in how they talk to or treat others. Can you see yourself caring more about that person than about yourself? If so, you should confront them about the way they are acting.

TASK: Write down what you would say to each person. Take one person each day for the next week and have that difficult conversation.

FACTOR – CRISIS PRONE

This construct describes the traits of people who tend to fill their lives with drama. They prefer to be emotionally upset. They may have a pattern of procrastination, waiting for the pressure of deadlines to motivate them to action. On the other hand, those who are not crisis prone have control over their emotional reactions. They are more thoughtful and organized. They are much better able to plan and to stick with their plan than are those who are easily distracted by their emotional distress, much of which, as we will see, is of their own creation.

SELF-ASSESSED RATING – TREADING WATER

You regularly encounter crisis but have a foundation that is reasonably stable and useful.

SESSION 1

EXERCISE 1A – CRISIS PRONE, TREADING WATER

Your life is stuck largely because of drama. While your life isn't getting worse, it isn't getting better either. You are allowing unnecessary emotional upset to get in the way of productive choices that would make your life stronger and better. You either aren't dreaming a bigger and better dream for your life or aren't willing to make the necessary choices to fulfill your dream. It is time to take responsibility for the price you are paying to live in drama.

TASK: List the implications of the drama in your life. How is it holding you back? What do you want that you don't have because of drama? Revisit this list every day for the next week and add to it.

EXERCISE 2A – CRISIS PRONE, TREADING WATER

Now you see that your life isn't progressing because of drama. You are caught up in enough unneeded turmoil to distract you from creating positive dreams for your life and/or executing on them. You are simply spending too much time on fruitless concerns to tend to more useful ones. It is likely that the drama in your life comes from limited sources. You may be involved in a relationship that is negative, complaining, or resentful. You may be too fearful to change jobs to one that is more fulfilling. It is now time to face whatever drama is holding you back.

TASK: Make a list of the drama in your life. Don't leave anything out. Revisit that list every day for one week and add to it.

EXERCISE 3A – CRISIS PRONE, TREADING WATER

While the drama in your life might come from limited sources, it is keeping you from building a more positive and powerful life. As you look at your list of dramas, which one seems to be the most important for you to address? Which seems to most stand in the way of the change you know you need to make? Which is blocking your dreams and/or forward progress?

TASK: After you identify that one, rank any others in terms of negative impact on your life. Revisit your list every day for the next week and reorder until you are clear they are ordered correctly.

EXERCISE 4A – CRISIS PRONE, TREADING WATER

You have identified the drama that is blocking your ability to dream a better dream for your life and to achieve it.

TASK: Now, it is time for you to consider how your life will be better when you have removed this drama from your life. How will your life be better? Where will you go? What will you do without this obstacle? Write it down and be specific. Allow the joy of your new energy and vitality to show up in your description. Imagining this change is the first step toward creating it. Reread your list every day and allow yourself to enjoy the positive energy of being free.

SESSION 2

EXERCISE 1B – CRISIS PRONE, TREADING WATER

Some people who are treading water in their lives are doing so because they are stuck in victim drama. They feel at the mercy of others and/or circumstances as if it isn't under their ability to make positive changes. They worry about the future so much that it undercuts the courage to move forward.

TASK: Create a list of where you are playing the victim. Be clear about each relationship and/or circumstances where you tend to hold back or pretend out of fear of negative consequences. Review your list every day for the next week and add more examples as you find them.

EXERCISE 2B – CRISIS PRONE, TREADING WATER

You can maintain the victim role only by having others play the villain and hero in your life. Perhaps, instead of taking full responsibility for treading water, you have blamed your circumstances on others or expected others to care for you in ways you should be caring for yourself. Doing so keeps you stuck because it gives you ways and reasons to avoid making the changes in your life you know you need to make.

TASK: Next to each victim drama on your list, write the names of those who are villains and heroes in your life. Review your list every day for the next week and add names to it.

EXERCISE 3B – CRISIS PRONE, TREADING WATER

You know how to stand up for yourself and your life in most circumstances. But, it is likely that if you are treading water, you have been too fearful of a few people or circumstances to liberate your life from their control. You know you aren't telling the truth because you fear the consequences. You know you aren't admitting to what you want to do because you think you might be criticized or unsupported. It is only when you are willing to stand up for yourself and your life that you will free yourself from feeling dominated.

TASK: Take one of the people you have put in the villain role and write what you need to say or do to end the drama between you. Be specific. Practice saying it out loud until it feels comfortable. Now, go and have that conversation.

EXERCISE 4B – CRISIS PRONE, TREADING WATER

You have been allowing others to fill in some of the gaps in your life that are your responsibility to address. Perhaps you have been coasting because you have others in your life who achieve enough for both of you. Regardless, it is your responsibility to live up to your abilities. It is time to face any dependencies you have created and to step out of them.

TASK: Make a list of any people on whose coattails you have been riding or any place where you are taking credit for that which you don't deserve. List next to each the responsibility you need to assume and do so. Take a week to complete these lists.

SESSION 3

EXERCISE 1C – CRISIS PRONE, TREADING WATER

Some people who are treading water in their lives are doing so because they are stuck in villain drama. They envy others and wish their lives were more successful but instead of doing the hard work of making changes, they find fault with those they envy and talk them down whenever they can. Where are you playing the villain? Do you find yourself gossiping about the problems and failures of others and getting some delight? Do you get angry when people don't treat you as if you are special? These manifestations of villain anger are likely holding you back from a more successful and happy life.

TASK: List all of the places and relationships where your negativity might be hurting someone who cares for you. Review your list every day for the next week and add more examples as you find them.

EXERCISE 2C – CRISIS PRONE, TREADING WATER

You can maintain the villain role only by having others play the victim and hero in your life. Perhaps you have done a reasonable job of concealing your judgments and negativity in places where it matters the most, like work. But your villain drama may be creating a ceiling effect that is limiting your ability to rise any higher in life. You simply can't create enough allies to continue to expand your success. People who get to know you better find you too unpleasant to form deep and lasting relationships. While some people might pretend to like you (victims) and others may make excuses for you (heroes), no one finds it easy to work with you.

TASK: Next to each villain drama on your list, write the names of those who are victims and heroes in your life. Review your list every day for the next week and add names to it.

EXERCISE 3C – CRISIS PRONE, TREADING WATER

While you certainly have some healthy and positive relationships in your life, it is likely that your villain drama is dominating a few key individuals or souring some of your opportunities. Hence, your life is a bit stuck. Those people might be pretending to like and support you more than they actually do, and you may be so occupied with your judgments and criticisms as to not notice.

TASK: Your task is to take notice and see who adapts themselves to you out of concern not to upset you. Take one of the people you have put in the victim role and practice making room for them to show up with greater candor and openness. Practice every day with this person and notice the changes that occur.

EXERCISE 4C – CRISIS PRONE, TREADING WATER

You have been allowing a few people in your life to excuse your lack of drive and ambition. You know your life has stalled and that you haven't done anything about it.

TASK: Make a list of those people who either feel sorry for you or who make it okay for you to settle for less than who you can be and what you can do. What do they say that excuses you from taking 100 percent responsibility for your full success? Go to each of them this week and thank them for the care they have shown you and then tell them that you don't want their kindness any longer. You are willing to accept the good and the bad that you create.

SESSION 4

EXERCISE 1D – CRISIS PRONE, TREADING WATER

Some people who are treading water in their lives are doing so because they created a level of comfort and are unwilling to challenge themselves to take on more. Being a hero to the people in your life invites them into a codependent relationship in which you agree to make excuses for each other. If you don't push them, they won't push you. If you put up with their lack of ambition, they will put up with yours. This hero drama can be subtle and seductive. You will see it by noticing if the significant people in your life are getting stronger or weaker from being in a relationship with you. Are their lives getting better or are they in decline?

TASK: List all of the significant relationships in your life. Next to each indicate if their lives are getting stronger (S) or weaker (W). See if you can identify your influence in either direction. Revisit your list every day for the next week and add insights.

EXERCISE 2D – CRISIS PRONE, TREADING WATER

You enjoy the hero role because it makes it less obvious that you are treading water if those around you are doing the same or are eroding. But heroes need victims or villains to maintain the drama. Some people you invite to be dependent on you and you excuse their unwillingness to push themselves. These are your victims. For others, you make excuses for their poor interpersonal skills. These are your villains. By not pushing them to be better, you avoid being pushed by them.

TASK: Revisit your list from the last exercise. Who are your victims? Who are your villains? Revisit your list every day for the next week and add insights.

EXERCISE 3D – CRISIS PRONE, TREADING WATER

Review your list of victims. Next to each name list how you are supporting them in avoiding taking on challenges that would strengthen their lives. What is the next step for them to take on their journey? What do they need to take on that they are avoiding? How could you encourage them to move forward and withdraw your acceptance of the status quo in their lives without wounding the relationship?

TASK: Take one person on your list and talk to them about their next step. Notice how it feels to support their growth.

EXERCISE 4D – CRISIS PRONE, TREADING WATER

Review your list of villains. Can you see how you are making excuses for the ways they are limiting their lives? You know they are doing things that make it almost impossible for them to get unstuck and to make their lives better. You might see them being judgmental and critical of others. You know others view them as difficult to be around but you join in or sympathize. Can you see the value you would bring to each of them by confronting them and inviting them to give up their bad behavior? Can you see how their lives would improve?

TASK: Make a list of what you would say to each person on your list. Take one person each day for the next week and have this powerful conversation.

FACTOR – CRISIS PRONE

This construct describes the traits of people who tend to fill their lives with drama. They prefer to be emotionally upset. They may have a pattern of procrastination, waiting for the pressure of deadlines to motivate them to action. On the other hand, those who are not crisis prone have control over their emotional reactions. They are more thoughtful and organized. They are much better able to plan and to stick with their plan than are those who are easily distracted by their emotional distress, much of which, as we will see, is of their own creation.

SELF-ASSESSED RATING – GROWING

You sometimes encounter crisis but have a foundation for your life that is strong.

SESSION 1

EXERCISE 1A – CRISIS PRONE, GROWING

Your life has been moving forward steadily, and you are doing well. But, you aren't fully at peace with yourself and the world around you. You have not yet broken completely free of drama. Perhaps you find yourself comparing yourself to others and taking some satisfaction from feeling better than others. Or, you may occasionally become attached to some outcome and are frustrated when things don't go your way. It is time to take on whatever is holding you back from thriving.

TASK: Take some time and list the price you are paying to maintain the drama in your life. Be specific. Revisit your list each day for the next week and add to it.

EXERCISE 2A – CRISIS PRONE, GROWING

Now you see that while you are growing, there is some drama that is limiting your ability to fully thrive. What is it? Write it down. Be specific. It may be a person in your life who stirs up jealousy or envy. It could be some circumstance that is less than optimal for you. Or, it could be something inside you such as a lingering anxiety or grudge. Your list might not be long, but this is the opportunity for you to identify that which is standing in the way of a real breakthrough in your peace and joy.

TASK: Revisit your list each day for one week and modify it to make it as accurate as possible.

EXERCISE 3A - CRISIS PRONE, GROWING

It is likely you have only a few sources of drama that are limiting your ability to thrive. Which one is your greatest obstacle? Give this some thought and write it down. Why do you maintain it? What do you get from keeping it in your life?

TASK: Answer these questions as clearly as possible and revisit your answers every day for the next week.

EXERCISE 4A – CRISIS PRONE, GROWING

Now it is time to envision how your life will be improved when you remove this drama from it. You have done a good job in caring for your life. Yet, this little drama is a bit like rowing a boat across a lake while dragging the anchor. It only makes things harder. How will it feel when you cut the anchor line and can row almost effortlessly? Be descriptive. Write freely.

TASK: Try to capture in your words the joy, peace, and purpose you will feel as you liberate your life from the last remnant of drama. Revisit your description every day for the next week and meditate on the vision you captured on paper.

SESSION 2

EXERCISE 1B – CRISIS PRONE, GROWING

You are growing because you don't allow much drama into your life. Not many people who are growing tolerate much victim drama, but even a little can hold you back from fully thriving. You are playing the victim when you aren't fully candid with others or when you hold yourself back out of the fear of whatever consequence you imagine would occur if you fully showed up.

TASK: Make a list of any ways you limit yourself by unnecessary worry and fear of potential outcomes. Review this list every day for the next week in order to add more insights.

EXERCISE 2B – CRISIS PRONE, GROWING

Whatever victim drama might be in your life creates others who show up as villains and/or heroes. If you don't choose to be fully candid because you fear making someone angry, you are placing them in the role of a villain. You fear their reaction and so aren't being your full self. If you fail to take full responsibility to be all you can be and then complain to someone that your gifts aren't fully recognized, you are making that person a hero in your life. They are letting you off the hook for your own decisions.

TASK: Using your list of victim dramas, name the people you are turning into villains and heroes in your life. Review the list every day for the next week and add names.

EXERCISE 3B – CRISIS PRONE, GROWING

For the most part, you are who you are. But, there might still be one or two places where you play the victim to the villain you have created. You are avoiding a conversation you know you need to have. You are putting off a decision you know you need to make. You are doing so because you are fearful of how someone will react to you. You don't want to face their anger, judgment, or resentment. Now, it is time for you to set yourself free. What will you need to say to that person? What decision do you need to make? What will you say when you have that conversation or announce that decision? Are you ready to be free?

TASK: Then, do it this week. Have the conversation or make that decision and announce it.

EXERCISE 4B – CRISIS PRONE, GROWING

You may have only one or two places where you are allowing others to take care of you when you should be taking care of yourself. These might be subtle like accepting compliments you don't deserve or not being called out on agreements you have not met. Regardless, it is time to throw off any dependence on the goodness of others that you don't deserve.

TASK: Make a list of any such dependencies and how you will now take responsibility for that aspect of your life.

SESSION 3

EXERCISE 1C – CRISIS PRONE, GROWING

You are growing because you don't allow much drama into your life. Not many people who are growing tolerate much victim drama, but even a little can hold you back from fully thriving. You are playing the victim when you aren't fully candid with others or when you hold yourself back out of the fear of whatever consequence you imagine would occur if you fully showed up.

TASK: Make a list of any ways you limit yourself by unnecessary worry and fear of potential outcomes. Review this list every day for the next week in order to add more insights.

EXERCISE 2C – CRISIS PRONE, GROWING

Whatever villain drama might be in your life creates others who show up as victims and/or heroes. You may be quite friendly and cordial most of the time, but any unresolved resentments may, from time to time, erupt on those around you. A dog doesn't need to bite more than once to be thought of as a biting dog. Even polite people who possess just a little villain energy will create victims who avoid being fully open with them and heroes who keep thinking they will change or make excuses for them.

TASK: Using your list of villain dramas, name the people you are turning into victims and heroes in your life. Review the list every day for the next week and add names.

EXERCISE 3C – CRISIS PRONE, GROWING

For the most part you are a respectful and reasonable person. But at times you might have a "big" personality that tends to demand the attention of others and takes up much of the air in the room. While you are productive and fair-minded, you may not be aware that your need to be recognized can overshadow others and put them in the position of being victims to your needs and wants. This might not seem to be an issue for you but can certainly result in not getting the very best from those with whom you work and live.

TASK: Your task this week is to practice making yourself small so that others can be bigger. Talk less and listen more. Ask about others more than you talk about yourself. In doing so, you may find you expand your power and freedom.

EXERCISE 4C – CRISIS PRONE, GROWING

There might not be many places where you invite people to be heroes in your life. But it is important that you seek to find any. Your best friends are those who see all of your potential and any and all ways you are failing to develop it. They are always encouraging you to be the best you can be. You may find a few people in your life are willing for you to settle for a little less than your best and who entice you to think it is okay to be less than fully thriving.

TASK: Make a list of those people. Go to each one this week and tell them your goal of being fully yourself. Ask for them to push you wherever they see you holding back.

SESSION 4

EXERCISE 1D – CRISIS PRONE, GROWING

Because you are growing, hero drama may be quite familiar to you. You are proud of your accomplishments. You know many of them have been earned only with significant effort and courage. You like feeling useful and important. It may be easy for you to magnify your feeling of being special by making life easier on those around you. You might be proud of their dependence on you because it shows how much you have to share. You may enjoy the patience you have with the people in your life who get in their own way because it indicates your level of maturity and accomplishment. But by playing the hero you are weakening people who need to get stronger.

TASK: List all of the key people in your life. Revisit your list each day for the next week and add insights.

EXERCISE 2D – CRISIS PRONE, GROWING

To the extent you are creating hero drama, you are weakening the important people in your life. In order to maintain the feeling of being more competent than your family and friends, you need to have others play the victim and villain role. Those who you invite to be dependent on you in order to escape taking responsibility for the challenges in their lives are your victims. Those who have blind spots for attitudes and behaviors that get in their own way and for which you make excuses or turn a blind eye are your villains.

TASK: Revisit your list from your last exercise. Who is acting as the victim? Who is acting as the villain? Revisit your list each day for the next week and add insights.

EXERCISE 3D – CRISIS PRONE, GROWING

Review your list of victims. Can you identify how you might be using their weakness to foster your own sense of value? Are you willing to give this up for their benefit? If so, what do they need to face in their lives that would make them stronger and more complete? What is the next step they need to take? Picture how it would feel to watch them give up a bad habit, take on a new job, move out on their own. Can you see yourself being proud of yourself for making their welfare more valuable than your feeling of being better than they are? Now, take action.

TASK: Pick one person on the list and have the right conversation. Pick a different person and do the same each day for the next week.

EXERCISE 4D – CRISIS PRONE, GROWING

Review your list of villains. Can you identify how you indulge even subtle missteps in your friends rather than confronting them on their blind spots? You may see that they are flirting with an affair but don't say anything because your marriage is stronger. You hear them talk about considering some unethical behavior at work but don't warn them of the danger. It is almost as if you might have some secret satisfaction if things go south in their life. It is time to give up your hero role.

TASK: Write down next to each name the issue you see that they need to address. Take one name each day for the next week and have the difficult conversation.

EXERCISE SERIES: AUTONOMOUS

FACTOR – AUTONOMOUS

Gaining personal freedom and giving up being needy.

SELF-ASSESSED RATING - HANGING ON

You are completely dependent on others for your security and stability.

SESSION 1

EXERCISE 1A – AUTONOMOUS, HANGING ON

Rate your life on the following scale: 1. Totally dependent on others for my survival, 2. Mostly dependent on others, 3. Moderately dependent on others, 4. Slightly dependent on others, and 5. Not at all dependent on others. There is no right or wrong answer here but it is important to be honest about the condition of your life. The more dependent you are on others, the less likely it is that you accurately see your capabilities or use all of your gifts to shape and grow your life. Consider how you feel about being as dependent as you are. How much motivation do you have to change?

TASK: Revisit your rating each day for the next week and see if you shift it either higher or lower.

EXERCISE 2A – AUTONOMOUS, HANGING ON

Make a list of all of the areas in your life where you lack freedom. Review your list every day for the next week and add any insights you have. Consider your situation at work. Do you feel free to be yourself in your job? Do you experience a feeling of being free at home? How about in your friendships?

TASK: Next to each area where you lack full freedom, write what is missing. Why don't you feel free?

EXERCISE 3A – AUTONOMOUS, HANGING ON

Make a list of all dependencies you have on substances or habits. These certainly should include things like alcohol and drugs, but should also include any habits that limit your freedom. You might be a workaholic or may watch too much television. You may not be fully aware of habits you have allowed to steal your freedom from you.

TASK: Revisit your list every day for the next week and add to it any other dependencies of which you become aware.

EXERCISE 4A – AUTONOMOUS, HANGING ON

You may or may not realize how habits of thinking become patterns that rob us of independence and foster neediness. Some of these may have started when you were quite young. Perhaps you weren't skilled at baseball and so now avoid all sports because you assume you have no ability. You have sacrificed your freedom to play and compete because of the pattern of shame you developed over your lack of skill in one sport. Take some time to list as many of these dependence patterns as you can identify. You may notice that they begin something like, "I can't do ________ because _______." Or, "I am no good at _____ because I couldn't do ________." Or, "I can't have what I want because ________." Every one of these dependence patterns limits your freedom and robs you of independence.

TASK: Review your list every day this week and add to it any new insights.

SESSION 2

EXERCISE 1B – AUTONOMOUS, HANGING ON

Critical to becoming less dependent and more independent is owning your successes. While your life might be in disrepair, you certainly have not failed at everything in your life. It is so important to carefully record whatever successes you have created throughout your life. Often, hidden within those events are clues to strengths and abilities that can be put to use today to expand your independence. Look back over your life and list every success you have had. When you are finished, look back over the list and identify common threads. What did you bring to those circumstances that allowed you to win? What gifts did you demonstrate?

TASK: Make a list of your strengths and abilities. Revisit that list every day this week and add to it.

EXERCISE 2B – AUTONOMOUS, HANGING ON

While hanging on in life is certainly not a pleasant experience, you may feel so trapped by your circumstances that you fail to notice the freedom you actually have. Viktor Frankl, a famous psychiatrist, noted that noticing and exercising even small freedoms can provide meaning to your life and provide a foundation for forward movement. No matter how bad your circumstances, you don't have to give up. You have the freedom to think your own thoughts, to dream dreams, and to make plans.

TASK: Play with this list. You can make it as long as you like, but the reason for compiling it is to give you the opportunity to smile about your circumstance and to feel some hope for your future. If you have some freedom, you could have more.

EXERCISE 3B – AUTONOMOUS, HANGING ON

Neediness, like freedom, is hardly ever absolute. Even little children resist their neediness and fight for greater independence. It is so important for you to take note of that which you do for yourself and the positive ways you care for your life and to take pride in those things. In every way that you take ownership of yourself and your life, you establish a base from which you can expand your independence. If your grades aren't good, you can still take pride in the fact that you go to almost every class. If you don't have many friends, you can take notice that you continue to be friendly. These are powerful observations.

TASK: Record all that you notice and keep your list growing through the week. Read it every day and allow yourself to be proud of whatever you are doing for yourself. Don't allow a critical voice in your head to diminish your actions and choices that are positive and empowering.

EXERCISE 4B – AUTONOMOUS, HANGING ON

Even when you are feeling powerless, you still have power. Just as you have noticed your successes, your freedom, and the ways you care for yourself, it is critical that you notice your power. Who listens to you when you talk? Who turns to you for advice? Who depends on you for their survival? Who calls you their friend? Whose lives do you contribute to in a positive way? What do you do that is productive and meaningful? Who do you care for? Who is in need of care? What do you give to others without looking for anything in return? Your acts and caring for others are huge expressions of your power. Just as a stone thrown into a pond sends out many ripples that continue to expand, your power is having impact on the lives of others that you may not fully see.

TASK: Make a list of all of the expressions of your power. Be as complete as you can. Review your list every day this week and celebrate yourself for the power you bring to your world.

SESSION 3

EXERCISE 1C – AUTONOMOUS, HANGING ON

For the next four weeks we are going to ask you to take on a skill with which you may be unfamiliar. It is called meditation. Meditation is simply a way of harnessing your thoughts for a positive gain. Your thoughts are important because they shape your behavior much more than you may realize. Your first exercise is to repeat this phrase to yourself: *I need no one but myself.* How does it sound when you say it? You may find it hard to believe. But, it is far truer than you know. Close your eyes and say it again. Do you begin to feel some empowerment? This exercise takes practice.

TASK: We want you to repeat this sentence five times each day for the next week. Allow it to take root in your life until you begin to see how it might be true.

EXERCISE 2C – AUTONOMOUS, HANGING ON

Now, we are asking that you add to last week's meditation a new concept: *I can be whomever I want.* Say it out loud. Now, close your eyes and say it three times. Can you believe that this might be true? Even though your life is currently in disrepair, you begin to regain ground when you believe it doesn't have to be this way. Your life is the canvas on which you will express yourself. And that starts with considering who you want to be.

TASK: As you spend the next seven days repeating this sentence and *I need no one but myself,* begin to consider who you might want to be. Write down whatever thoughts come to mind.

EXERCISE 3C – AUTONOMOUS, HANGING ON

This third week we are adding a new thought to your meditation: *I can do whatever I want to do.* Your current life might not feel like it contains a lot of freedom, but it doesn't have to be constricting. Say it out loud, "I can do whatever I want to do." Close your eyes and repeat it three times. What comes to mind that you might want to do that you currently aren't doing? Write it down. At this point, you don't have to be reasonable or practical. Just give in to the power of those words.

TASK: Repeat them to yourself five times each day for the next week. Keep a record of all that you want to do that you currently aren't doing.

EXERCISE 4C – AUTONOMOUS, HANGING ON

Finally, we have one more thought to add to your meditation. This may be the most challenging of them all: *I can have whatever I want.* This might not be the story of your life, but our goal is to expand your freedom and independence. As you say this to yourself, *I can have whatever I want,* pay attention to the thoughts that come into your mind. How have you been limiting yourself? How have you surrendered your desires and accepted your circumstances without a fight?

TASK: As you repeat this sentence five times each day for the next seven days, let the power of those words begin to give you inner freedom to reach for more.

SESSION 4

EXERCISE 1D – AUTONOMOUS, HANGING ON

Now you are ready to begin to expand your independence. Today's exercise is about the power of choice. Every day you make hundreds of choices, some big and some small. Your choices are either a manifestation of your neediness or of your independence. You get to choose.

TASK: List the choices you have already made today. Which ones expressed neediness and which expressed independence? Pick choices you will make today to expand your independence. The size of the issue is inconsequential. It is important only that the choice reduces your neediness and expands your independence. For example, you may depend on others to wake you up in the morning. Now, you can choose to wake yourself up.

EXERCISE 2D – AUTONOMOUS, HANGING ON

Every expansion of freedom starts with a declaration that sounds something like this: *I am tired of being oppressed and will rebel to have my freedom.* It is very important that you declare your intention to expand your freedom wherever you feel it is constrained. For example, you may feel like you aren't free to be your full self in your job. No one seems interested in your ideas so you gave up sharing them. But, now you want more independence. You want your ideas to matter. Your declaration would be to create your job in a way that your ideas are valued and put to use. Wherever you want more freedom and independence you need a declaration.

TASK: So, take some time and write out your declaration of independence. Be comprehensive. Reread it a few times to make sure it captures all of your thoughts. Now, share it with the important people in your life.

EXERCISE 3D – AUTONOMOUS, HANGING ON

You have declared your independence. Now, you need to claim it. Whatever vision you have for your more independent life will be achieved only when you change the rules of the game. It is up to you to create a clear vision of the more independent life you want to have. Be specific and clear. *I want a marriage where I am honored and respected. I want to be financially independent. I want to be able to take care of myself. I want to have a job I love.* Once you are clear about your independence, it is your job to begin making those things a reality. Take the one that is easiest to achieve and create an action plan. What will you need to do first? What do you need to do next? How quickly can you move through your plan?

TASK: Write it out and put it in action.

EXERCISE 4D – AUTONOMOUS, HANGING ON

Being more independent doesn't mean you don't have meaningful relationships where people share responsibility for tasks. Interdependence is very different from dependence. Dependence means you can't get along on your own. Independence means you don't need anyone. Interdependence occurs when you can stand on your own two feet and invite others who are also independent to join you in moving forward. Most of the accomplishments we create in life require the collaboration of independent people in interdependent relationships.

TASK: Now that you have your action plan to become more independent, list the people who are resources to assist you in moving forward. Share your plan of action with them and ask them to join you.

FACTOR – AUTONOMOUS

Gaining personal freedom and giving up being needy.

SELF-ASSESSED RATING - ERODING

You are dependent on others in many, but not all, areas of your life.

SESSION 1

EXERCISE 1A – AUTONOMOUS, ERODING

Rate your life on the following scale: 1. Totally dependent on others for my survival, 2. Mostly dependent on others, 3. Moderately dependent on others, 4. Slightly dependent on others, and 5. Not at all dependent on others. There is no right or wrong answer here but it is important to be honest about the condition of your life. The more dependent you are on others, the less likely it is that you accurately see your capabilities or use all of your gifts to shape and grow your life. Consider how you feel about being as dependent as you are. How much motivation do you have to change?

TASK: Revisit your rating each day for the next week and see if you shift it either higher or lower.

EXERCISE 2A – AUTONOMOUS, ERODING

Make a list of all of the areas in your life where you are losing freedom. You may notice that you used to have greater independence, but, for some reason, it is slipping away from you. You may have taken pride in your career but now feel at the mercy of a job you don't like. Or, you may have had a mutually satisfying marriage that has devolved into a relationship filled with secrets and manipulation. You may have seen yourself as competent in many ways but now are becoming filled with self-doubt.

TASK: Noticing the trends where you are losing your independence is important because it helps you to see where you need to work on your life.

EXERCISE 3A – AUTONOMOUS, ERODING

Make a list of habits you have developed that are undermining your independence and freedom. Some habits start out to be harmless but gradually creep into patterns that weaken you. You may have gotten used to a glass of wine at dinner that now is a habit of drinking the rest of the evening. You know you have a weakening habit when you can't seem to stop it. Rather than controlling the habit, the habit is controlling you.

TASK: As you make your list, notice your resistance to write things down because you don't want to face them. You may be saying to yourself, *This isn't all that bad*. If so, add it to the list. You wouldn't be having that thought if it wasn't an issue you need to address.

EXERCISE 4A – AUTONOMOUS, ERODING

Notice how you relate to the people in your life. To whom have you sacrificed your freedom? There are some clear signs of eroding autonomy in relationships. You find yourself calibrating what you say because it doesn't feel safe to simply say what is on your mind. You notice that you modify your behavior when you are around some people. You don't laugh when you think something is funny or show when your feelings are hurt or you are angry. Such constrictions of freedom in relationships often increase over time unless they are addressed, leading to even greater loss of freedom.

TASK: Make a list of relationships where you have limited freedom.

SESSION 2

EXERCISE 1B – AUTONOMOUS, ERODING

Session 2 invites you to see some of the ways that your lack of autonomy is creating erosion of your life. Let's get started. Exercise 1 invites you to see how you are starting to fall behind. Life requires a certain pace of growth. When you don't keep up with that pace, you can see the signs you are beginning to fall behind. You may notice the people around you accomplishing things that you aren't accomplishing. Your friends are talking about things you know nothing about. You haven't learned anything new in quite some time. All of these are signs that you are beginning to fall behind. Your lack of autonomy is showing up as you see yourself falling behind the pace of the people around you and know not only will you not win the race, you are falling further and further behind. This is not a good feeling but it is an important one to face.

TASK: Make a list of the evidence that you are beginning to fall behind.

EXERCISE 2B – AUTONOMOUS, ERODING

Exercise 2 invites you to see that not only are you falling behind but you aren't growing. Growing is obvious in the new things that are coming into your life. These include new thoughts, new feelings, new friends, new experiences, and new opportunities. When you can't identify much that is new, you should begin to face the reality that your autonomy is eroding.

TASK: Make a list of everything that is new in your life over the last few months. Now, look at that list. Some of the things on your list might be quite trivial. Hopefully, some things are quite profound. Notice if you have too few new things to have a life that is thriving.

EXERCISE 3B – AUTONOMOUS, ERODING

Exercise 3 invites you to see that you are becoming progressively dependent on others. This is not always easy to see because autonomy can be surrendered gradually over time. The evidence of becoming progressively dependent is that you are doing less on your own and are progressively leaning on others for support, encouragement, and help. It is most helpful when you can see that you are depending on people in your life to do things for you that you can do for yourself.

TASK: Make a list of all that you depend on others to do for you. Now, look at that list. Circle each item where you are depending on someone to do something for you that you can do for yourself.

EXERCISE 4B – AUTONOMOUS, ERODING

Exercise 4 invites you to see that you are progressively becoming weaker as a person. You might remember times in the past when you were courageous, independent, bold, and adventuresome. But now when you look at your life you can see that you are more frightened, timid, reluctant, and hesitant. You may not realize how you got there, but with reflection you can see that the choices you have made have not made you stronger but have instead made you weaker.

TASK: Make a list of the evidence that your life is weaker than it used to be. Be courageous in making your list and review it each day for the next week.

SESSION 3

EXERCISE 1C – AUTONOMOUS, ERODING

Session 3 focuses your attention on gaining greater autonomy in your thoughts and feelings. Your inner life is the source of all life change. Until you gain greater autonomy here, no outward change can be sustained. Let's get started. Exercise 1 invites you to deal with your fear. Everyone experiences fear. It is a natural part of life and signals some threat to your well-being. You can see your life eroding and it creates fear. Until you arrest the decline, bad things are in store for you. When fear is too great, it can lead to paralysis instead of action. You simply can't afford to bury your head in the sand and hope things will work out. You need to listen to your fear so you can take action. What are the threats?

TASK: Write them down. Prioritize them from the most immediate and serious to the least immediate and least threatening. Simply ordering them is the first step of getting in the fight for your life.

EXERCISE 2C – AUTONOMOUS, ERODING

Exercise 2 invites you to feed hope. Hope is no more than projecting a positive outcome onto your life. Hope is not about certainty. You don't know that your hope will materialize. But, hope gives you something to focus on, something concrete to work toward that is preferable to your current situation. While you know your life is eroding, you can hope that you are on solid ground. Imagine what that would look like. You might hope to have a job that provides you with more than enough money and is satisfying. You might hope for a meaningful and stable relationship. You can hope for anything. Hope allows you to rise above the paralysis of fear and to get to work creating something good.

TASK: Make a list of three to five things that you can hope for in your life.

EXERCISE 3C – AUTONOMOUS, ERODING

Exercise 3 invites you to focus on your strength. Strength is necessary to turn hope into reality. Change isn't easy for anyone. It will require work. Work requires strength. You may not be feeling particularly strong since your life has been eroding, but don't fool yourself; you are stronger than you think. If you look into your past, you will find things that you fought for and won. You will find times when you persevered when things were challenging and difficult. You will find times when you stood up for things that were important to you. Each of these is evidence of your strength. You need to see your strength more clearly so you can call on it when you need to take on a challenge.

TASK: Make a list of times when you were strong.

EXERCISE 4C – AUTONOMOUS, ERODING

Exercise 4 invites you to focus on your courage. Courage is the ability to take on challenges without backing down, to keep believing in a better future even when things are hard, and to keep moving when you are discouraged. Courage allows you to persevere. The challenge before you is to move from eroding to treading water. You must break the trend you are on in order to get to a better place. This will require courage.

TASK: Look back over your life to times when you demonstrated courage. You may have surprised yourself and others when you rose to a challenge no one thought you could take on. These times are important because they remind you that you can be amazingly courageous. List every one.

SESSION 4

EXERCISE 1D – AUTONOMOUS, ERODING

Session 4 focuses your attention on outward changes you can make in your autonomy to move your life from eroding to at least treading water. Let's get started. Exercise 1 invites you to identify the issue you need to address first. When you are eroding, you can sense things aren't going well. You know you need to do something or else face worsening conditions. But to change things, you will first need to clearly identify the most important issue to address. If your ship is sinking, the life jackets and pumps are important, but the most critical issue is to plug the leak. Once you plug the leak, no more water will enter your boat. You can begin to recover. Unless you plug the leak, nothing else will matter very much. So, what is the biggest leak in your boat? It could be your situation at work that has been making you unhappy, frustrated, and angry for years. Or, it could be your marriage that constantly drags you down. Or, you might be grossly overweight and feel overwhelmed by your health situation. While you might have many issues going on, you must pick only one as the most important leak to address.

TASK: Write it down and review it every day.

EXERCISE 2D – AUTONOMOUS, ERODING

Exercise 2 invites you to identify your oppressor. You scored low on autonomy because you have surrendered your life to someone or something else. Instead of being yourself, you are conforming to the expectations of another person or situation. You are viewing the situation as if you can't be free. This dynamic can start in a very subtle way and then grow until it overtakes your life. You may be in a relationship with someone who seems needy, and so you become their caretaker. At first, you feel good about yourself for being able to help. But the person you are helping never seems to get any better. Instead, their needs grow. You are now resentful of the care you are giving that is restricting your life but feel trapped in the need to keep providing care. You have gotten yourself into a situation where you are oppressed by the needs of this person.

TASK: Identify the one oppressor to which you have sacrificed your autonomy. It might be a person or a situation.

EXERCISE 3D – AUTONOMOUS, ERODING

Exercise 3 invites you to regain your voice. You may now notice that you have many thoughts about your oppressor that you rarely, if ever, share. You might feel trapped, frustrated, and angry but you are fearful that saying such things out loud would only make things worse and create a bigger burden for you. Hence, you keep your thoughts and feelings to yourself. Recovering and expressing your voice is critically important in expanding your autonomy. You can practice by writing down whatever is on your mind. Don't hold anything back. Now, read it out loud. Notice any anxiety you have about simply hearing your true words spoken out loud.

TASK: Read your words out loud every day for the next week to practice getting comfortable with your voice.

EXERCISE 4D – AUTONOMOUS, ERODING

Exercise 4 invites you to break free. This may not be easy, but it is necessary if you are to transition from eroding to treading water. Breaking free requires that you speak your voice, all of it, to the person or situation where you are allowing yourself to be oppressed. This could be to your boss, your spouse, or to your best friend. It might be to your bad habit or health situation. You must be willing to side with your autonomy over whatever might occur from speaking your truth. You could lose your job. You might lose a close relationship. But those losses are necessary in order for you to be more of who you really are. You had to clear the deck in order to find a better situation—one that fit your life.

TASK: Take action and write down how you would break free.

FACTOR – AUTONOMOUS

Gaining personal freedom and giving up being needy.

SELF-ASSESSED RATING - TREADING WATER

You are dependent on others in only a few areas of your life but none that are required for stability.

SESSION 1

EXERCISE 1A – AUTONOMOUS, TREADING WATER

Rate your life on the following scale: 1. Totally dependent on others for my survival, 2. Mostly dependent on others, 3. Moderately dependent on others, 4. Slightly dependent on others, and 5. Not at all dependent on others. There is no right or wrong answer here, but it is important to be honest about the condition of your life. The more dependent you are on others, the less likely it is that you accurately see your capabilities or use all of your gifts to shape and grow your life. Consider how you feel about being as dependent as you are. How much motivation do you have to change?

TASK: Revisit your rating each day for the next week and see if you shift it either higher or lower.

EXERCISE 2A – AUTONOMOUS, TREADING WATER

You are treading water because you lack sufficient autonomy to grow. You may be focused more on being safe than on growing. Growing requires letting go of security in order to take more risks and have new experiences that expand autonomy. While you might not consider yourself an overly dependent person, you might find numerous examples of ways you play it safe and depend on the familiar and comfortable instead of forging new and different paths for yourself.

TASK: Make a list of ways you play it safe and choose security over growth and change. Review your list every day for the next week and add insights.

EXERCISE 3A – AUTONOMOUS, TREADING WATER

Fears are another way you might be avoiding autonomy. You may have a very active imagination with regard to all that can go wrong if you move forward into unfamiliar territory. You know how to get along in your current circumstances. But if you take on new challenges and greater independence, you face greater possibility of discomfort, embarrassment, and failure. Your active mind may exaggerate those fears to such an extent that you are unwilling to take on anything new. You might pass on a new job opportunity because it will require gaining new skills or working with new people. You might be unwilling to move because you fear not getting along with new neighbors or learning your way around a new location. Exaggerated fear can greatly undermine your autonomy.

TASK: Make a list of all of your fears. Can you discern which are realistic and which are not? How are they holding you back from growing?

EXERCISE 4A – AUTONOMOUS, TREADING WATER

Dependency is another way you might be avoiding the autonomy necessary for growth. You may "hook" people into caring for you in ways you can care for yourself but make you feel loved and valued. Such codependency might seem cute and tender but it has a dark side. In order to perpetuate such a dependency, you must keep acting needy. Instead of becoming more self-sufficient and self-reliant, you must play the weakling. You may also not see that your neediness turns your friend into a caregiver, someone who now sees you as someone who requires assistance to get by. Over time, this perspective undermines respect and true love.

TASK: Make a list of any dependent relationships you currently have and the benefit you derive from each one.

SESSION 2

EXERCISE 1B – AUTONOMOUS, TREADING WATER

Session 2 focuses your attention on evidence that your lack of autonomy is resulting in your life treading water.

Exercise 1 invites you to see that you are stuck in the ordinary. Your life is likely okay. There is nothing wrong. But, you might notice that your life hardly ever changes. You are in a rut. You have deep-seated habits about how you spend your time, who you hang out with, what you talk about, and what you do. They aren't bad habits, but they prescribe almost everything you do. They don't allow for much change. See if you can make a list of your habits. These are all of the things you do without thinking about them or making decisions.

TASK: Notice how they define your life.

EXERCISE 2B – AUTONOMOUS, TREADING WATER

Exercise 2 invites you to see how little new comes into your life. This isn't always easy to see because you become used to life as it is. But if you pay attention, you may notice that not much has changed in your life for quite some time. You haven't formed a new friendship, changed the style of your hair, traveled to a new place, or gained a new skill. The lack of things new is a sign of having surrendered your autonomy.

TASK: Make a list of all of the new things you have added to your life over the last three months. If you don't have much on your list, consider what that means about your need for greater autonomy.

EXERCISE 3B – AUTONOMOUS, TREADING WATER

Exercise 3 invites you to see that you have only modest ambition. Perhaps you used to dream of big things like being rich, wildly in love, or changing the world. But for quite some time your dreams have been about just maintaining what you have. You may not realize that your dreams have shrunk over the years. Small ambitions don't require much autonomy. You can achieve them without much change. You can be cheating yourself by lowering your expectations to make things easy.

TASK: Make a list of your dreams and then evaluate how ambitious they are.

EXERCISE 4B – AUTONOMOUS, TREADING WATER

Exercise 4 invites you to see that you have a reluctance to change. You may find yourself making excuses about why you don't need to change. Perhaps you say to yourself you have changed enough in your life. You are at a stage of life where you don't need to learn new things. You have accomplished enough; it is now time to enjoy what you have done. All of these are excuses that allow you to avoid the responsibility to continue to expand your autonomy and to continue to grow.

TASK: Make a list of the excuses you use to avoid the responsibility to continue to grow.

SESSION 3

EXERCISE 1C – AUTONOMOUS, TREADING WATER

Session 3 focuses your attention on gaining greater autonomy in your thoughts and feelings so you can move from treading water to growing. Your inner life is the source of all life change. It is only when you have strengthened your thoughts and feelings that you can master your life challenges. Let's get started.

Exercise 1 invites you to confront contentment and the lethargy that comes with it. It is easy to reach a place where you are comfortable and then to lose the motivation to keep moving forward. You have a good life. You don't have any major problems. Why keep pushing for greater autonomy when things are good? This is the question that undermines growth and expansion. Look for evidence that you have become content with aspects of your life. Lethargy and contentment can show up in all areas of life. You might be content with your physical state even though you are overweight and out of shape. You can be content with your career and are resting on your laurels. You may be content in your marriage and so aren't investing in developing it.

TASK: Make a list of all of the areas where you have accepted contentment with how things are.

EXERCISE 2C – AUTONOMOUS, TREADING WATER

Exercise 2 invites you to consider the value of curiosity in expanding autonomy. Curiosity is a natural part of life. Children are curious about almost everything. Perhaps it is unfortunate that as we age, many people seem to lose some of that natural curiosity that drives exploration and change. Consider what you are curious about. What do you want to learn that you don't currently know? Where do you want to visit that you haven't been? What experiences are on your bucket list? Curiosity is a powerful motivator to shake you out of contentment because it pushes you to explore.

TASK: Get in touch with your curiosity by making a list of things you want to know, do, experience, and explore.

EXERCISE 3C – AUTONOMOUS, TREADING WATER

Exercise 3 invites you to consider the value of challenge. Challenge pits you against opportunity. It requires that you test your skills and expand them where necessary. All challenges, regardless of their nature, are helpful in expanding autonomy. If you enter a race, you will push yourself to run faster than your competitors. If you enter a spelling contest, you will test your memory and your ability to retrieve information. If you enter an art contest, you will expand your creativity. Challenges are healthy ways to grow. You can challenge yourself without entering contests by simply considering how you can be more efficient, effective, faster, better, or smarter today than you were yesterday. This week practice finding and creating challenges for yourself every day.

TASK: Notice the impact on your autonomy.

EXERCISE 4C – AUTONOMOUS, TREADING WATER

Exercise 4 invites you to see the value of excitement to expand your autonomy. Excitement is an emotion that naturally occurs in everyone. It is wise to pay attention to your excitement because it naturally releases energy into your life to make things happen. If you are excited to attend the concert that is coming to town, you will find out how to get tickets, invite some of your friends, and schedule your time so you can attend. You will create an event for yourself that isn't part of your regular status quo. You will have a new experience that will likely contribute to your growth and expansion. It is important to feed your excitement by noticing where it naturally occurs and then to find ways to put it into action.

TASK: Make a list of any things that are currently exciting you. Consider how you can turn them into real plans and action.

SESSION 4

EXERCISE 1D – AUTONOMOUS, TREADING WATER

Session 4 focuses your attention on outward changes you can make in your autonomy to move from treading water to growing as a person. Let's get started. Exercise 1 invites you to notice if there are any particular individuals with whom or situations in which you tend to limit your autonomy. You may find you are more freely yourself in some places and with some people than with others. This is an important observation because it allows you to identify patterns in which you are prone to hold back and to not be your full self. Give this some thought and make a list of places, situations, or people around whom you don't fully express yourself.

TASK: Now, look at your list. What causes you to hold back? Write down your answer.

EXERCISE 2D – AUTONOMOUS, TREADING WATER

Exercise 2 invites you to practice taking note of and expressing your preferences. It is likely common for people to ask you what you want for lunch, where you want to go for dinner, or what movie you want to see.

TASK: Pay attention to how often you say something like, "It doesn't matter. What do you want?" This is one place where you can concretely practice expanding your autonomy. First, simply notice if you have a preference. If you truly don't, it is fine to say so. Second, if you do have a preference, even if it isn't all that important to you, practice stating it. "Actually, I would like a ham sandwich for lunch." "I would like to try that new Thai restaurant that just opened at the mall." "I have been waiting to see that new action movie." Stating your preference isn't the same as insisting on getting what you want. It is a way of showing up more fully.

EXERCISE 3D – AUTONOMOUS, TREADING WATER

Exercise 3 invites you to practice being candid. This exercise is an expansion of the last one. When you are in conversation, notice when you are holding back on your opinion, thoughts, or judgments. You might be disagreeing with the person with whom you are speaking. Or, you may have something to add. Or, you might be having some judgment about the person who is speaking. How often do you express your thoughts versus keeping them to yourself? An important part of autonomy is expanding your willingness to be candid. Practice noticing what you are thinking and finding as many ways as possible to introduce your thoughts, opinions, and judgments into the conversation.

TASK: Notice the impact on your autonomy.

EXERCISE 4D – AUTONOMOUS, TREADING WATER

Exercise 4 invites you to practice being creative. Creative self-expression is another expansion of autonomy. You can choose to bring more of your creativity into all that you do. You don't have to conform to the expectations of those around you. You can choose to do things your way. You may decorate your cubicle at work in such a way that more of your uniqueness becomes apparent to your coworkers. You may interact with people in new and different ways because you want to. You may choose to dress more creatively or cook more creatively. Putting your spin on even ordinary events in life is a way to expand your autonomy and self-expression.

TASK: List five ways you could be more creative at home and at work this week.

FACTOR – AUTONOMOUS

Gaining personal freedom and giving up being needy.

SELF-ASSESSED RATING - GROWING

You are, for the most part, free of dependence on others except in one or two areas.

SESSION 1

EXERCISE 1A – AUTONOMOUS, GROWING

Rate your life on the following scale: 1. Totally dependent on others for my survival, 2. Mostly dependent on others, 3. Moderately dependent on others, 4. Slightly dependent on others, and 5. Not at all dependent on others. There is no right or wrong answer here but it is important to be honest about the condition of your life. The more dependent you are on others, the less likely it is that you accurately see your capabilities or use all of your gifts to shape and grow your life. Consider how you feel about being as dependent as you are. How much motivation do you have to change?

TASK: Revisit your rating each day for the next week and see if you shift it either higher or lower.

EXERCISE 2A – AUTONOMOUS, GROWING

You have sufficient autonomy to be growing, but not enough to be thriving. Let's explore some of the ways you might be limiting your autonomy. One of the things that limits autonomy is making things more important than your own life and growth. We call these your sacred cows. Sacred cows can be almost anything. You may want your parents to admire you and so are unwilling to do things they wouldn't understand and accept, even though you know you are doing nothing wrong. You might not want to risk losing your marriage and so hold back on some of your ambition, creativity, or talent. Whatever you put ahead of your growth can become an obstacle to autonomy.

TASK: Make a list of your sacred cows. Review your list every day for the next week and add items.

EXERCISE 3A – AUTONOMOUS, GROWING

A second inhibitor of the autonomy you need to thrive may be the lack of awareness of your full potential. If you don't have an accurate view of your true giftedness, you can easily set goals that aren't sufficiently high and so don't require your full autonomy to achieve. One way to observe this problem is to notice how often you fail. If you succeed at everything you do, it is likely you are shooting too low. If you are truly challenging yourself, from time to time you will stretch too far and find yourself unable to reach your goal. These failures are healthy and suggest you are pushing yourself to the fullest.

TASK: Make a list of the failures you have experienced and see how many come from pushing yourself too far. If you have a very short list, you can assume you either don't see your giftedness accurately or don't push yourself hard enough.

EXERCISE 4A – AUTONOMOUS, GROWING

A third inhibitor of the autonomy you need to thrive is the lack of courage. It takes courage to keep moving forward in life—leaving behind the old and pressing forward into the new. Everyone gets scared from time to time. The difference between those who are growing and those who are thriving is that thrivers take fear as a signal to move forward instead of standing their ground. Courage enables you to overcome fear and to move forward with boldness. Take some time to assess your courage.

TASK: List five times when you have seen your courage in action and five times when you lacked sufficient courage to overcome your resistance.

SESSION 2

EXERCISE 1B – AUTONOMOUS, GROWING

Session 2 focuses your attention on how the limitations in your autonomy limit your ability to thrive. Let's get started.

Exercise 1 invites you to notice that you are willing to accept limitations. While it is important to you to grow, you are also willing to accept limitations. Your life is good. In many ways it is better than the lives of your friends and family. To get to the next level, you would have to sacrifice some of that which you value about the life you have. You are unwilling to let go of what you have for what you could have. This is such an easy temptation for everyone. But it will limit your life.

TASK: Make a list of the ways you are settling for what you have and not pressing forward for what you could have.

EXERCISE 2B – AUTONOMOUS, GROWING

Exercise 2 invites you to see that you are accepting being less than you could be. This is a subtle difference from Exercise 1 but it is a profound one as well. You have a responsibility to be all that you can be, to use your gifts as fully as they can be used. You may be successful enough that you aren't willing to push for the more of who you could be.

TASK: See if you can find evidence that you have settled for being less than who you could be. Ask people who know you well if they see evidence of this in your life.

EXERCISE 3B – AUTONOMOUS, GROWING

Exercise 3 invites you to see if you are being unwilling to be unique. If you hold back just a little bit on who you are, you can fit in and be acceptable to others. If you are fully committed to being your autonomous self, you must be willing to stand out and be different. The world doesn't always accept those who are different. Yet different is powerful.

TASK: See if you can find evidence that you have held back on being your unique self in order to avoid conflict or rejection. Who might you be if you threw off social expectations and the fear of rejection?

EXERCISE 4B – AUTONOMOUS, GROWING

Exercise 4 invites you to see if you have been unwilling to break the rules. Rules are important. They create order in society. But breaking the rules is sometimes the only pathway to be unique, special, and powerful. Sometimes the rules that need to be broken are only to social mores of your family or social group. But, they can exert a strong control. In order to be your full self, you must be willing to walk your own path even if it is not understood or accepted by others.

TASK: Where are you holding back on your journey because you are unwilling to break rules?

SESSION 3

EXERCISE 1C – AUTONOMOUS, GROWING

Session 3 focuses your attention on some inner work you may need to do before you experience the autonomy you need to shift from growing to thriving. All change happens on the inside before it manifests on the outside. Let's get started.

Exercise 1 invites you to master the acceptance of your uniqueness. It might be a bit trite, but you are as unique as a snowflake. That is a very big thought. There is no one exactly like you and there never will be. Your uniqueness is something to notice and embrace. It means there is a special expression of your life that is yours to find. You can't thrive until you are committed to finding it. You aren't like everyone else. You aren't like anyone else. What is it about you that is completely unique?

TASK: See if you can write that down. How do you feel about this idea? Does it excite you or scare you? Spend this week contemplating your uniqueness and what it might mean for how you should live your life.

EXERCISE 2C – AUTONOMOUS, GROWING

Exercise 2 invites you to take on the idea of aloneness as a positive quality for expanding autonomy. You have many friends and some with whom you are very close. Perhaps you have a very intimate relationship that you call your soulmate. But part of thriving is the acceptance that your life is essentially and fundamentally yours and can't be shared with anyone. It is your life to live. There is aloneness in life that, if resisted, makes full autonomy impossible. You can describe your experiences to your friends and soulmate but no one will experience them like you did. Your experience of life is unique.

TASK: This week notice your fundamental aloneness and see if you can embrace it more fully. Notice how it impacts your sense of autonomy.

EXERCISE 3C – AUTONOMOUS, GROWING

Exercise 3 invites you to notice wonder in the world around you. Wonder is a concept that expands your experience of all of life. The simplest things are opportunities for vast wonder. You see a bird on your walk to work in the morning. You notice its color and wonder about the subtleties in it and how different birds are colored differently. You wonder about the experience of flying and what it must be like. You wonder about the manifestation of life itself in the bird. How does that come to be? All of this wondering can occur just from noticing an ordinary bird. Wondering draws you out of yourself into a bigger world.

TASK: Practice wondering every day this week. Notice the impact it has on your autonomy.

EXERCISE 4C – AUTONOMOUS, GROWING

Exercise 4 invites you to pay attention to intimacy in your life. Intimacy is the experience of knowing and being known. It requires paying close and deep attention to someone or something and letting yourself be genuinely and openly known. Intimacy expands autonomy because it is the sharing of your uniqueness that feeds it. If you pay attention to your relationship with intimacy, you may begin to identify some of the ways you hold yourself back from some of the expansion of your life. You may find yourself unwilling to know things about the people in your life or unwilling to allow some things about yourself to be known. If so, it is here that you are limiting your thriving.

TASK: This week notice your relationship to intimacy and where you might set limits on it.

SESSION 4

EXERCISE 1D – AUTONOMOUS, GROWING

Session 4 focuses your attention on concrete external changes you can make that will encourage the autonomy you need to move from growing to thriving. Let's get started. Exercise 1 invites you to throw off any constraints that are limiting your full self-expression. It is likely that you are being your full self in most circumstances. But, you may find that there are one or two places where you are holding back. And, you may not realize that holding back in those few places is limiting your autonomy elsewhere. It is time for you to throw off those constraints and to value your freedom more highly than maintaining the status quo in those situations.

TASK: Make a list of those few places where you are allowing yourself to be constrained and resolve them this week. Notice the impact on your autonomy.

EXERCISE 2D – AUTONOMOUS, GROWING

Exercise 2 invites you to take big risks. You have likely taken many risks in your life, believing in yourself and your ability to create what you want. We are encouraging you to push the envelope even more. Few people express all they have to give to the world. There are so many things that signal caution and so many people who encourage holding back for safety's sake. Our message is quite the opposite. Put yourself on the line every day. Look for ways to take bigger risks every day. Take risks in what you say, what you want, and how you do things. Risks challenge your growth as well as challenging those around you.

TASK: List five risks you could take today.

EXERCISE 3D – AUTONOMOUS, GROWING

Exercise 3 invites you to be different. Each of us is different in a multitude of ways. Very few people express their differentness as much as they could (and perhaps should). Your differentness is the composite of your unique way of seeing the world, your preferences, and your creativity. It is likely that when you are expressing your differentness you won't ever be the way anyone expects you to be. You won't ever say what others expect you to say. People will experience you as always interesting, surprising, and novel. The more you practice expressing yourself in new and unique ways, the more your autonomy will shine.

TASK: Practice each day over the next week adding your uniqueness to everything you say and do. Notice the impact it has on your autonomy.

EXERCISE 4D – AUTONOMOUS, GROWING

Exercise 4 invites you to do things your way. This exercise is similar to but not the same as Exercise 3.

Exercise 3 focused on showing your uniqueness. This exercise invites you to powerfully influence the world around you to adapt to your thoughts, plans, and visions. You are not on the earth simply to be yourself but also to shape how things occur. Your unique perspective and creativity provides you with great wisdom as to how things could work better. Exerting your influence on the people and situations in your life should be a creative project that creates greater good.

TASK: List five ways you could influence your world to be even better. Now put them to work.

EXERCISE SERIES: PLEASING

FACTOR – PLEASING

Give up pleasing others as a life strategy in order to better come to know what is unique and special about you.

SELF-ASSESSED RATING - HANGING ON

You seek to please others in every situation because you are completely dependent on their goodwill.

SESSION 1

EXERCISE 1A – PLEASING, HANGING ON

Your life is in disarray partly because you have a deep-seated pattern of doing everything to please others and completely ignoring your own needs and wants. You have hoped that by winning the favor of others, they will take care of you but you are discovering that the opposite is true. People stop caring for you and view you as more of a problem rather than someone who is useful and truly helpful. This first exercise asks you to see if you can clearly assess how much this is true of your life.

TASK: Rate yourself 1-3 on the following scale: 1. I try to become what everyone wants me to be and have no clue who I am, 2. I try to please almost everyone but do have some times when I care for myself, and 3. I have patterns of pleasing those whom I think I need, but have some relationships where I express my wants and wishes.

EXERCISE 2A – PLEASING, HANGING ON

It is likely that you have been pleasing others all of your life. Take a few minutes to think back to your childhood. Who wanted you to please them?

TASK: Make a list. Why was it important to them to be pleased? Notice the pull they exerted on you to think about their needs rather than your own. Write down how you feel as you think about this now.

EXERCISE 3A – PLEASING, HANGING ON

Perhaps there were a few times when you wanted to rebel or to do something that wouldn't please the people who were raising you. These may have been your first efforts at breaking free from pleasing. Think through your early years.

TASK: Make a list of everything you can think of that were examples of your effort to do your own thing, to do what you wanted to do. Revisit this list every day for the next week and add others that come to mind.

EXERCISE 4A – PLEASING, HANGING ON

Take out your list from last week. What happened when you tried to rebel or establish some independence? It is likely that for some reason you gave up and/or retreated. See if you can remember how that happened to you. What happened? Were you frightened into giving up? Were you enticed into backing down with promise of some reward?

TASK: Think through each of these events and imagine how your life might have been different if you hadn't backed down but had moved forward instead.

SESSION 2

EXERCISE 1B – PLEASING, HANGING ON

We will ask you to take the next month to assess where you please others in various aspects of your life. This is important because the more clearly you can see your pattern of pleasing, the more likely it is that you will be able to break free of it. Let's get started. Where in your family of origin do you please instead of being yourself? Do you find yourself telling your mother that you love her when you aren't feeling love? Do you visit your father because you want to avoid his anger or the feelings of guilt he gives you? Consider your mother, father, sisters and brothers, aunts, uncles, cousins, and grandparents.

TASK: Make a list and review it every day for the next week.

EXERCISE 2B – PLEASING, HANGING ON

Now, focus the same exercise on your immediate family. Do you try to please your spouse to avoid conflict or to get the attention you want? Do you try to please your children in order to be liked or to get them to cooperate?

TASK: Think through each relationship and make a list of the people you manage by trying to please them. Review this list every day for the next week and add to it any new insights you have.

EXERCISE 3B – PLEASING, HANGING ON

Consider your workplace. Who do you try to please at work? You may find that you pretend to be who you are not when your boss is around so she likes you. You may try to please coworkers in the hope that they are cooperative with you or include you in their social group. You may be trying to please people who report to you. Think it through.

TASK: Make a complete list.

EXERCISE 4B – PLEASING, HANGING ON

Finally, consider people in your neighborhood, social circle, or school. Do you have friends whom you try to please in order to maintain their friendship? Do you have people in your neighborhood you cater to because you are fearful of their displeasure? Perhaps you have teachers or professors whom you manage by pleasing and pretending.

TASK: Take the next week to make a complete list. Review your lists of people you are pleasing. It might be a very long list. Consider the impact this is having on your life.

SESSION 3

EXERCISE 1C – PLEASING, HANGING ON

Now, we want to shift your focus on the ways that you please. You may be completely unaware of the things you do to please others. Let's get started.

TASK: Make a list of the things you say that aren't sincere. Look at your list of people you please. To whom do you lie in order to get along? Whom do you flatter?

EXERCISE 2C – PLEASING, HANGING ON

Secondly, where do you withhold what you think? Go through your list of people you please.

TASK: Write down any instances you can recall when you were thinking something that you were unwilling to say because you knew that person wouldn't want to hear it. You held back to avoid their imagined displeasure. Work on this every day for the next week.

EXERCISE 3C – PLEASING, HANGING ON

This week we want you to focus on things that you do that you don't want to do for the people in your life. You do these things to please others even when it doesn't please you. You may watch television shows you don't like but won't do anything about it. You may take on jobs at work that you don't want to do. You may watch your friend's dog because you are unwilling to say no.

TASK: Work on this list every day for the next week.

EXERCISE 4C – PLEASING, HANGING ON

In Exercise 4, hopefully you will be able to get in touch with many things that you would like to be doing.

TASK: Finally, make a list of the things you won't do because you are afraid to displease the people in your life.

SESSION 4

EXERCISE 1D – PLEASING, HANGING ON

Finally, we want you to come to see the price you have been playing for trying to please others as the primary means of building your life. You may not have noticed that it is simply not working. In fact, your life has been getting worse and worse while you have been hoping that pleasing others will lead to better outcomes.

TASK: Review the list of people you have been pleasing. Next to each name write what you have been hoping they would do for you. Be specific. Take the entire week to complete this project.

EXERCISE 2D – PLEASING, HANGING ON

Take out your list from last week. How many of those things you have been hoping for have actually happened?

TASK: Review your list carefully and write down next to each person's name whether or not you have gotten back what you had expected. If you are honest, you should notice that you have not. You have been hoping for a long time. Meanwhile, your life has been declining.

EXERCISE 3D – PLEASING, HANGING ON

Now, it is time to assess what you could have been doing for yourself that you have not because you have been counting on pleasing to work. What is the most immediate need in your life to begin to get it in order? Be careful here. This is an important decision. You might need a job because you were counting on others to support you. You might need more income at work and have been hoping for years that pleasing your boss would lead to a promotion. You might need companionship and have been hoping that pleasing your spouse would change him.

TASK: Get clear about that most important thing. Write it down.

EXERCISE 4D – PLEASING, HANGING ON

Stop pleasing in that one place that you identified last week. Take responsibility to get what you want regardless of how the people in your life feel about you. Be willing to rebel against their expectations in order to do what you need to do for your life.

TASK: Write down what you are going to do. Do it this week. Don't put it off.

FACTOR – PLEASING

Give up pleasing others as a life strategy in order to better come to know what is unique and special about you.

SELF-ASSESSED RATING - ERODING

You tend to please others because you fear rejection and their displeasure.

SESSION 1

EXERCISE 1A – PLEASING, ERODING

Your life is declining because you have been too dependent on trying to please others instead of depending on yourself to build your life. While you have some areas of independence, your efforts to please others take up too much of your time and energy and distract you from more beneficial choices. Our first series of exercises is designed to make you more aware of how frequently you use pleasing others as a primary tactic to get what you need for your life.

TASK: Make a list of the major areas of your life. This could include work or school, home, friendships, family members, etc. Rank them from highest to lowest in terms of where you think you please the most. Review this list every day for the next week and make adjustments.

EXERCISE 2A – PLEASING, ERODING

Now, focus your attention on work or school. Where do you find yourself pleasing others and where are you being yourself? You may find that in many places you express your desires and thoughts, but in some relationships you tend to try to read what others want from you and to adapt to their expectations.

TASK: Make two lists—one where you are adapting and one where you are being yourself. Review this list and add to it every day for the next week.

EXERCISE 3A – PLEASING, ERODING

Repeat the previous exercise with your attention on your family life. Pay attention to how you relate to your grandparents, in-laws, spouse, children, aunts, uncles, and cousins. With which ones do you cater to their needs while ignoring your own, hoping that pleasing them will lead to something you want or need? Perhaps you find yourself seeking love, or approval, or security by going along with someone's agenda. Or, you find yourself fearful of displeasing someone you care about.

TASK: Go through all relevant family members and list the ones you seek to please and those with whom you feel free to be yourself.

EXERCISE 4A – PLEASING, ERODING

Finally, repeat this exercise with your friendships and associations outside of work. This list would certainly include friends but also neighbors, club members, and others with whom you regularly associate. Perhaps you find yourself pleasing to be accepted or to avoid being rejected. You know you are pretending to be who you are not. With other people you express yourself openly and fully.

TASK: Make two lists and write names on each. Review this list every day for the next week and make changes.

SESSION 2

EXERCISE 1B – PLEASING, ERODING

Session 2 is focused on getting a better understanding of why you are pleasing. Let's face it. You learned to please as a child and you were rewarded for it. But as you got older, pleasing became less useful and actually detrimental. Instead of gaining independence, learning new skills, and developing greater competence, you relied on your old skills of pleasing in the hope that things would get better. But, it hasn't been working. In fact, your life has been getting progressively weaker. We want you to see clearly what you have been hoping to get out of pleasing others. Start by listing anything that comes to mind.

TASK: Answer this question: *Why do I please people in my life?* Write down whatever comes to mind. Review this list and add to it each day for the next week.

EXERCISE 2B – PLEASING, ERODING

Now, we want you to focus on what you hope to gain. Pleasing is always a strategy to get something or to avoid something. When it is being used to get something, it is because you view someone else as having something you want and/or need. It is your hope that if you make them happy enough, they will give it to you. The problem here is that you are starting from the place of making others big and you small. They are the ones who have, and you are the needy one. That is not a place of power.

TASK: Review your lists from Session 2. Write next to each name all of the things you might hope to get by pleasing. Be honest with yourself. Review this list every day for the next week and add insights you gain.

EXERCISE 3B – PLEASING, ERODING

If it isn't to gain something that causes us to please, it is because we hope to avoid something. Perhaps you are fearful of making someone mad or disappointing them because you view them as having the power to hurt you, make you feel guilty, or punish you in some other way. Your pleasing is a means of managing that threat. If you don't act like you like your friend, she will freeze you out of her social circle. So, you play along. We hope you are beginning to see that pleasing distracts you from seeing your capabilities. It limits your ability to get what you need for yourself.

TASK: Again, go through your lists from Session 2 and write down all of the threats you are trying to avoid by pleasing. Take your time. Review your list each day for the next week and make corrections.

EXERCISE 4B – PLEASING, ERODING

Finally, note that the strategy of pleasing others allows you to avoid taking responsibility for solving your own problems, getting what you need, and taking care of yourself. One of the things you might be seeking to gain from pleasing is to be cared for, to be sheltered by someone rather than sheltering yourself. You might be seeking someone else's friends rather than winning your own. Trying to remain dependent can drive pleasing behavior.

TASK: For the last time, review your lists from Session 2 and write down any dependencies you might be trying to maintain by pleasing. Review your list every day for the next week and add insights.

SESSION 3

EXERCISE 1C – PLEASING, ERODING

What is gained by not pleasing others? Just the idea might seem offensive to you. Of course, it is a good thing to make others happy. Why should I not? In this session we want to help you see clearly the reasons you may want to move past pleasing in your life. Pleasing is a lot like riding on the coattails of others. The people around you may have accomplished a lot. Your boss may have created a successful business. Your friend might have built a big social network. Your spouse might be a very loving person. You can see the abundance of those around you and you want it for yourself. That is natural. But getting it by enticing them to give it to you short-circuits the learning you need to get.

TASK: Notice where you might be trying to please others into giving you what they earned because they like you. Make a list of all of those places where you are playing this game. Can you see that this strategy will never make you as strong as you could and should be?

EXERCISE 2C – PLEASING, ERODING

Another reason you may avoid giving up pleasing is because it is safe where you are. You don't have many challenges or problems, because by pleasing you have people to take care of you and provide for you. Your husband makes plenty of money. Why should you develop a career? Your dad is running a family business. Why not take over for him when he is ready to retire? Who cares if you have no interest in the business? It makes plenty of money. Often, throwing off pleasing means giving up your security to find your own path. While it feels good to feel safe, you know you are giving up your self-esteem in exchange. Your life is getting weaker because you are depending on others.

TASK: Make a list of all of the places where you are holding on to things that weaken you. Review this list and add to it every day for the next week.

EXERCISE 3C – PLEASING, ERODING

Walking away: A third reason you may avoid giving up pleasing is that you would be walking away from a pretty cushy situation. There are many people who greatly desire to be pleased and will reward those who do so, even when it isn't deserved. By "buttering up" your teacher you might get a grade you didn't deserve. By flattering your boyfriend you might get taken to that fancy place for dinner. By sucking up to the boss he might excuse your mistake. Not pleasing is like walking out on all of these favors and standing on your own two feet. Who wants to do that when you can be taken care of? But notice that you are pretending to be who you are not instead of being who you are. You are making more of others than they deserve and making less of yourself than you deserve.

TASK: Make a list of all of the places you please because it is easy and comfortable for you.

EXERCISE 4C – PLEASING, ERODING

The final obstacle to giving up pleasing may be the harsh reality of starting on your own. You may be in a dead marriage, but you are too fearful of starting over, so you endure the emptiness for as long as you can. You may hate your job and know it is a dead end, but you won't quit because it is safe. You are simply too fearful to walk away. You don't know that the step of walking away is a step toward finding your own power. It is only when you walk away from those things you are holding on to that you will find your true power and purpose. It can be a terrifying thing to walk away. It can take great courage.

TASK: Make a list of all of those relationships and places where you know you need to walk away regardless of the cost. Be courageous. Review this list each day for the next week and add to it.

SESSION 4

EXERCISE 1D – PLEASING, ERODING

You should now have a pretty good idea of how you are undermining your life by trying to please others. You know where you are pleasing and why you are doing so. It is time now to do something about it. You don't have to change everything at once. But you need to start your journey. Thinking about change isn't the same thing as changing. Thinking about giving up pleasing is not the same thing as giving it up. Your first exercise is to clarify your first step. What is the first, and most important, place for you to give up pleasing in order to claim your life? Only you can make this decision. It is likely to be the place you fear going the most. You may hear the voice in your head saying, "You know you have to quit your job." Or, "You know you have to walk away from this marriage." Or, "You know you have to tell your mother that you don't like telling her that you love her whenever she calls." You can feel that this is a big step. Something will shift when you do it.

TASK: Write it down.

EXERCISE 2D – PLEASING, ERODING

Face your fears. It is okay to be scared. Fear is something you either run from or face. Today is the day to face it. What is the worst thing that can happen if you stop pleasing the person you identified in the last exercise? What might they do? What might happen? What is the worst possible scenario?

TASK: Write it down. Don't hold back. Write down your worst possible fears. Review this every day and let yourself be afraid.

EXERCISE 3D – PLEASING, ERODING

Consider the alternative. What happens if you continue to please? Look at where your life is headed. Can you see the price you are paying for pretending rather than being yourself? If you stay on the course you are currently on, where will it lead? How much longer can you afford to try to please to get what you want?

TASK: Write down where you are headed and where your life will be in one, five, and ten years if you don't change. Be clear and honest. Read this every day for the next week.

EXERCISE 4D – PLEASING, ERODING

Act. You know the risk. You see the benefit. Now it is time to act. Write down what you will say to the person you have been pleasing that will be your declaration of independence. You haven't been honest. You have been avoiding speaking up. You have been pretending to be who you are not.

TASK: Put that into words. Write it down. Practice saying it in front of the mirror and revise it until it sounds honest and completely sincere. Now, say it. Whatever happens will happen. You will be on your journey toward a better life.

FACTOR – PLEASING

Give up pleasing others as a life strategy in order to better come to know what is unique and special about you.

SELF-ASSESSED RATING - TREADING WATER

You are committed to expressing yourself in many ways but often please others.

SESSION 1

EXERCISE 1A – PLEASING, TREADING WATER

You are treading water in your life because you are depending on pleasing others in places that limit you from making your life stronger. You know how to take care of yourself in many ways. You have proven the ability to break free of dependencies in order to make your own decisions and actions. But in order to move forward, you must face some challenges that you have been avoiding. The purpose of these exercises is to assist you in identifying those places, to understand the reasons you are holding yourself back, and to equip you with the tools you need to break through. Let's get started.

Consider why your life is stuck. If you are honest, you will be able to identify the area fairly quickly. Perhaps you know you are at a dead end in your job, but you haven't done anything about it. Or, you are in a bad relationship and have been hoping it would change for a long time. Or, perhaps you aren't making the money you want to make.

TASK: Write down whatever comes to mind. There may be multiple areas you need to address. Make a list and review it every day for the next week. Add to it until it is complete.

EXERCISE 2A – PLEASING, TREADING WATER

Go back to your list and clarify who you have been trying to please that has kept you stuck in each of these areas. You scored low in this area because you have been hoping someone would resolve these issues for you instead of taking ownership to solve them yourself. Who are those people?

TASK: Write down names.

EXERCISE 3A – PLEASING, TREADING WATER

Return to your list. How have you been trying to please the people whose names you wrote down? You may have been pretending to like them more than you do. Or, you might not have been saying what you want. You may have been withholding resentment in the hope they would think you were more on their side than you are. You may have been putting up with their requests for things you didn't want to do.

TASK: It is very important that you become clear about how you have been seeking to please. These behaviors may have become almost second nature to you even though they have been weakening you. The more clearly you see them, the more powerfully you can change them.

EXERCISE 4A – PLEASING, TREADING WATER

Finally, return to your list and notice the feeling inside of you as you read through the things you have done to seek the goodwill of the people on your list. Can you see how you have been unhappy and/or resentful? Perhaps you can notice passive-aggressive behavior where you have subtly acted out your resentment by pretending to go along while secretly undermining or frustrating the other person. Your spouse may have asked you to pick up milk and eggs for the hundredth time when she was just in the store. You find yourself bringing home only the milk and saying they were out of eggs when you know it wasn't true.

TASK: Write down all of the negative feelings and behavior you can identify. This is all wasted energy. You could have been using your creativity and power to move forward in your life if you had broken free of pleasing.

SESSION 2

EXERCISE 1B – PLEASING, TREADING WATER

Session 2 is focused on facing your resistance to giving up pleasing. You aren't crazy. You know that pleasing could pay off. It just hasn't yet. And, even though you have been hoping for the payoff for a long time, it always might be right around the corner. This is one of the big reasons people avoid breaking free. It is like buying a lottery ticket in the hope of getting rich. It is possible but it is not a good strategy. How many people spend years in the futile attempt to change their spouse into someone they could like being around because they would rather keep hoping than face the alternative?

TASK: Review your list of people you are pleasing. Where have you been hoping for some change for a long time and secretly know you need to give up hoping and move on? This could be in your job, your home, your friendships, or any other place where you are stuck.

EXERCISE 2B – PLEASING, TREADING WATER

A second place where you might be resistant to giving up pleasing is the fear of negative consequences. You may know that breaking free of pleasing will not come without negative consequences. Again, you aren't crazy. In fact, you are probably correct. Change is often painful. Often life requires us to take one step backward before we can take two steps forward. You may really like your house and know that you will have to sell it if you get divorced, and so you keep trying to please your partner in order to keep the relationship going. You are simply too fearful of having to start over. Or, while you might hate your job, you don't believe you could find another one. You lack faith in yourself to believe you can do better. This is not uncommon.

TASK: Please make a list of all of your fears that may limit you from giving up pleasing in those places where you are stuck.

EXERCISE 3B – PLEASING, TREADING WATER

The first tool we want to give you in order to give up the pleasing behavior that has limited your growth is dreaming. The power of a positive dream can overcome the resistance of your fear of change. If you can envision clearly a better situation than the one you are in now, you are more likely to give up sustaining it. If you want a better job, what would it be? If you wish you had more money, how much do you want? If you wish your friend was nicer to you, what would nice look like? Dreaming a dream means not being practical. It is about siding with whatever you want and picturing it as if you had it.

TASK: Take each day of the next week and write down your dreams. Keep this to yourself. Don't hold back. Get in touch with all that you want for your future.

EXERCISE 4B – PLEASING, TREADING WATER

The second tool for change is being disgusted. You may know the story of the boiled frog. It jumped into cold water and was quite content. The water got warmer ever so slowly and the frog adapted to the changes. Eventually the water got so hot that the frog boiled to death. It is possible to get so used to the wishing and hoping of pleasing that you don't realize how much you are sacrificing in the hope that things will get better or the fear of change.

TASK: Make a list of all of the opportunities you have missed while you were hoping that pleasing those few people in your life would work out. Perhaps you passed up on some job offers or had someone who was really kind show interest in you. But you passed them up because you would have put at risk the pleasing relationship you have been maintaining.

SESSION 3

EXERCISE 1C – PLEASING, TREADING WATER

A third tool in giving up pleasing is to shift your hope for the future from depending on someone else to believing in yourself. Pleasing others as a means of creating success completely undervalues and underestimates your ability to take care of yourself. It is only when you depend on yourself that you will ever come close to achieving your potential. Giving up dependencies is a critical step in expanding your power and influence. You have done a lot for yourself. It is time for you to review all of the dependencies you have abandoned and to realize that every time you took such a step, your life grew stronger.

TASK: Make a list of the times you rebelled, stepped out of dependence, or took control of a new aspect of your life. What was the result? How did it work out?

EXERCISE 2C – PLEASING, TREADING WATER

Now it is time to begin to take action. We want you to focus on the most fundamental relationship in which you need to give up pleasing. You probably know which that is, even if you don't want to face it. You might be tempted to consider an easier one, or one that is not as impactful on your life. But, we want you to be courageous here. Which is the most important? Which one will get you unstuck so you can move forward in your journey toward thriving?

TASK: Write it down.

EXERCISE 3C – PLEASING, TREADING WATER

The next action we want you to take is speaking up. What will you say to this person to liberate you from pleasing?

TASK: We want you to write two lists. First, what are the things you have wanted to say to this person that you have been unwilling to say? Write down everything. Don't hold anything back. Next, what are the things you have withheld saying because you were too fearful of the consequences. These might seem the same and certainly can have some overlap. But, we want you to clean out everything you might have been withholding out of your desire to please. Now that you have listed everything, write down what you need to say to this person to give up pleasing. It might be something like, "I have not been being honest with you for a long time. While I have been trying to be nice to you, secretly I have been resentful and afraid of you."

EXERCISE 4C – PLEASING, TREADING WATER

Now that you have spoken up, it is time to rebel. Rebellion is a natural response to being oppressed. Our country was established by rebellion. Rebellion usually follows some kind of declaration of independence. It is not uncommon for children to rebel against their parents when they feel their freedom to be themselves is being impinged upon. Rebellion requires throwing off whatever fear has constrained you and breaking free to be who you want to be and to do what you want to do. It is both frightening and exciting all at the same time.

TASK: Make a list of how you would like to rebel against your current circumstances. Be descriptive and complete. Allow your words to excite you into action.

SESSION 4

EXERCISE 1D – PLEASING, TREADING WATER

Rebelling from the pleasing pattern that entrapped you will likely lead to some sort of rejection. You won't be valued as you had been. You will be forced to give up some sort of security or something that you valued. You may be view by others as "bad" because you disrupted the status quo. You must be willing to accept rejection as part of the process of rebellion and freedom and so a necessary step in establishing a fully thriving life.

TASK: Make a list of those places where you expect to be rejected for your rebellion. As you read through the list find acceptance. Make it okay for you to be rejected in order to find your life.

EXERCISE 2D – PLEASING, TREADING WATER

Part of rejection is the realization that you are alone. You have lost the support on which you depended. This can be quite startling and frightening at first. You had been reliant on the pleasure and goodness of others. Now, you are by yourself. There is no one to please. There is no one to whom to go for support. It is now all about you. We encourage you to turn this from a negative to a positive experience. Since it is just you, you can do whatever you want. You are now free to make your own choices. You are now unencumbered by the need to please anyone. You can decide what you will do with your new freedom.

TASK: Make a list of the most important things to do to get your life moving in the right direction.

EXERCISE 3D – PLEASING, TREADING WATER

Put the past behind you. Don't bother looking back at those you have left behind. You may be pressured to return into the old patterns you have now taken such risks to avoid. This can be especially tempting if you hit some bumps in the road and things don't go as smoothly as you may have thought. You need to know that the past holds nothing good for you. You must keep your focus ahead of you. You can create whatever you want for yourself but you must keep moving forward. Don't let discouragement, fear, or difficulty stop you. You only need to move forward one small step at a time.

TASK: List the next few steps you need to take.

EXERCISE 4D – PLEASING, TREADING WATER

Since your life is now yours to create, return to your list of dreams. Turn your dreams into a visual representation that you look at every day. Perhaps you cut out pictures from magazines to make your dreams more visual. Post them on your refrigerator or some other place that you will regularly see them.

TASK: A few times every day look at your dreams and imagine that you already have them. Use your dreams to motivate you to move forward boldly.

FACTOR – PLEASING

Give up pleasing others as a life strategy in order to better come to know what is unique and special about you.

SELF-ASSESSED RATING - GROWING

You are quite committed to being yourself but have a few relationships where you find yourself pleasing others rather than expressing yourself.

SESSION 1

EXERCISE 1A – PLEASING, GROWING

Since you are growing, it is likely that you have learned to give up pleasing in almost every part of your life except for one or two. But, those one or two relationships are holding you back from fully thriving. These exercises are designed to assist you in identifying those few relationships and equipping you with the insight, motivation, and tools to set yourself free. Let's get started. The first step in change is being honest about where you are. Can you see where you are still pleasing someone in your life at the cost of your full freedom and power? If so, write down who that is.

TASK: If not, review this exercise every day for the next week and look for places where you are being fully yourself.

EXERCISE 2A – PLEASING, GROWING

It is so important that you understand what you are getting from pleasing. As you grew and matured as a child, you put off things that held you back in order to continue to become more independent. You put off crawling in order to walk. You gave up wearing diapers. You gave up the security of your family to form friendships in the world. Wherever you stopped moving forward it is likely you did so because you valued what you were getting from the relationship as better or more than you could get for yourself. Sometimes people marry someone of wealth or accomplishment because they want the security or resources and don't believe they could create it for themselves. Or, they depend on the reputation of their work in the absence of forging their own reputation.

TASK: Write down what you are getting from the person you are pleasing that is so important to you.

EXERCISE 3A – PLEASING, GROWING

It is also possible that by pleasing you have been avoiding something that you fear. Perhaps you maintain your job only by pleasing your boss. Or, the only way you can keep your spouse interested in you is by pretending to support him when, in fact, you have no respect for him at all. You are simply too fearful of the consequences that might come from giving up pleasing.

TASK: Write down any insights you have into your anxiety and fear about giving up pleasing.

EXERCISE 4A – PLEASING, GROWING

Now, consider what you might actually be able to do for yourself if you gave up this pleasing relationship. No longer needing to pretend to be who you are not or to do what you don't want to do, you can now go after that which you have been hoping to be given by the person you have been pleasing. If you have been hoping to be valued by your spouse, if you give up pleasing, you will be free to find someone who truly values you.

TASK: Write down exactly what it would look like to get what you have wanted for so long.

SESSION 2

EXERCISE 1B – PLEASING, GROWING

Now consider what it would be like to face the thing you have been fearing and avoiding by pleasing. You might lose the security you have been working so hard to hold onto. Or, you might lose the job that you had hoped would be the platform for your success for such a long time. Can you see past your fear? Can you see that your fear has kept you from facing the challenge and held you back from moving on? Imagine facing that thing you have been fearing and then taking the next step beyond your fear.

TASK: Write it down. Do you feel the excitement of being free?

EXERCISE 2B – PLEASING, GROWING

Have a tough conversation. You may consider reading *Fierce Conversations* by Susan Scott. Ms. Scott encourages her readers to learn how to step into conversations they may have been avoiding but need to have. She talks about facing reality and addressing it with your words. For you, this might mean speaking directly to the person you have been afraid to displease and having an honest conversation about how you have not been honest and have held back on some of your thoughts and feelings.

TASK: If so, have that conversation.

EXERCISE 3B – PLEASING, GROWING

Next, learn to monitor all of your words. When are you not being completely candid? Keep a log this week of every conversation where you either held back some of your thoughts or said things you didn't completely mean. Do you see that even though you might think you are only being polite, you are actually managing the relationship rather than showing up and accepting whatever might occur? These occurrences might be subtle but it is a good habit to notice each one and to prompt yourself to say whatever you need to say.

TASK: Practice this and you will avoid falling into any traps of pleasing.

EXERCISE 4B – PLEASING, GROWING

Being candid isn't usually enough to break free of pleasing. Typically, there is some action you must take to free yourself. You are doing something that you don't really want to do but feel required to in order to maintain your relationship. You may work for a difficult person who really enjoys talking because he likes to think he is very smart. You actively listen, and, even though you have better ideas, you don't share them because you don't want to pop his bubble. Now it is time for you to speak up and, in a respectful way, share your thoughts. You simply can't be as powerful as you were meant to be if you are playing second fiddle to someone who is less capable than are you. It may create some disruption for you to act, but it is important.

TASK: Write down what you need to do and when you will do it this week.

SESSION 3

EXERCISE 1C – PLEASING, GROWING

Next, notice where you might not be taking action because you are afraid. We could use the same example as last week. Your boss might be full of himself and likes to hear himself talk even when what he says isn't useful. You know you have better ideas but are fearful of being fired if you speak up. How long will you live under this type of intimidation? Isn't it time for you to believe in your ideas and in yourself? You really don't know what will happen when you show up. You might be fired. Or, you might be promoted. Something will likely change. It is this change we are looking for. It is time for you to bring more of what you have to bring to the world around you.

TASK: Write down what you are afraid to do and put it in play this week.

EXERCISE 2C – PLEASING, GROWING

Now practice being in action in every moment of every day. Pay attention to your feelings. When you allow your thoughts, wishes, and agendas to be overlooked or undervalued by others, you may notice some irritation, even if it is minor. You might feel your mood darken and may feel a bit angry. This is the sign of some small act of pleasing that you are not dealing with. If you don't correct the situation, you might notice that you begin to act out with passive-aggressive behavior, being sarcastic or a bit snippy.

TASK: Keep a list of any of these instances that you encounter this week. Review your list every day and begin taking action to correct the situation as soon as you notice it.

EXERCISE 3C – PLEASING, GROWING

You are now freeing yourself from every place where you are pleasing others. The next step in your growth is to notice if people in your life are trying to please you. You will notice pleasing behavior if you sense that people aren't being fully candid with you, that they are holding back or saying things they think you want to hear.

TASK: Make a list of all of the people you relate to who seem to be pleasing you. Review this list every day for the next week and add names.

EXERCISE 4C – PLEASING, GROWING

Review your list from the last exercise and have a conversation with each person on your list. Tell them that you sense they might be pleasing you either because they want something from you or fear the consequence of not winning your favor. Assure them that you are committed to their welfare regardless of how they act toward you and that you most want them to be fully themselves around you.

TASK: Ask if you do anything that encourages them to please you. Take responsibility for any way you invite them to please you and stop it.

SESSION 4

EXERCISE 1D – PLEASING, GROWING

Releasing people from pleasing is a great first step. Now, it is time for you to be aware of how you can empower others. Empowering people requires you to notice their unique skills and gifts and to look for every opportunity to encourage them to bring more of themselves into the open. Look for every way to give responsibility to others even when you could discharge it more quickly and efficiently yourself.

TASK: Make a list of any opportunities that come to mind. Practice this week giving the people around you more responsibility to act.

EXERCISE 2D – PLEASING, GROWING

You can use your freedom from pleasing to form more powerful alliances in the world around you. Your freedom allows you to align with other people who have given up pleasing and to form relationships where neither holds back from the other. Partnerships such as these are exceptionally powerful because they unleash the uniqueness of all participants. It is in these partnerships that 1+1=3.

TASK: Make a list of the people you know who might be powerful allies. Reach out to those people and add them to your personal network.

EXERCISE 3D – PLEASING, GROWING

Now that you are forming a robust network of powerful allies, how can you unleash the power of this group? Powerful people need a mission. How do you want to express your purpose through your network? Consider the causes that are important to you.

TASK: Make a list. How could your network extend or expand your causes if you invited them to participate using their unique skills and abilities? Once you are clear, invite your network, wherever appropriate, to join you in accomplishing your mission. This is the greatest expansion of getting free from pleasing.

EXERCISE 4D – PLEASING, GROWING

It is always wise when you have completed a journey to stop, look back, and appreciate the process. You started on this path because your life was constricted in some way by your habit of pleasing. You were holding on to some vestige of an attitude and behavior that was limiting your full thriving. Along the way you gained some insights and new skills that have allowed you to resolve whatever issue was holding you back. Take some time to appreciate yourself.

TASK: List the lessons you learned while on this journey and consider how you will use them as you move forward in your life.

EXERCISE SERIES: PRETENTIOUS

FACTOR – PRETENTIOUS

Give up pretending to be who you aren't and whatever success you have by pretending in order to find your true source of strength and power.

SELF-ASSESSED RATING - HANGING ON

Your whole life is built on what you are pretending to be rather than on who you really are. You have no idea who you are.

SESSION 1

EXERCISE 1A – PRETENTIOUS, HANGING ON

You believe your own pretense. Pretending to be what you are not and taking credit for what you don't deserve has been undermining your life. While it might have seemed like a good strategy, it is our hope that you will open your eyes to how it has actually undermined you.

Session 1 is designed to help you gain awareness of your level of pretending. The lower the level, the more you need to wake up and face the reality of what you are doing to yourself. You are at the lowest level (Level 1) if you don't even know that you are pretending. It might be unlikely that you are at this level since you have read the Circle and have completed the assessment, but be open to the fact that you might be pretending far more than you are aware. If you are at Level 1, own it.

TASK: Over the next week, ask five people who know you well and who will be honest with you how much they think you pretend to be who you are not. Be open to their answers.

EXERCISE 2A – PRETENTIOUS, HANGING ON

You know you are pretending but think it is okay. You are at Level 2 if you know you are pretending and you think it is a reasonable strategy. You may have achieved some successes and/or some security by pretending in the past and still believe that this is a useful way to build your life. Your task is to face how those around you have caught on to your pretense and have stopped believing in you. They now see you are a pretender and a fake. They don't trust you and so have withdrawn from you because you have not been honest.

TASK: Make a list of the relationships you have lost because you have been pretending.

EXERCISE 3A – PRETENTIOUS, HANGING ON

You know you pretend and understand the cost. You are at Level 3 if you know you pretend and are becoming aware of the price you have paid. You are beginning to see that because you didn't earn what you received, you did not gain the skills necessary to move forward in your life. Because you took credit from those who deserved it, you have lost relationships that were valuable and would be very useful to you now.

TASK: Make a list of all of your regrets. Review this list every day for the next week and allow your feeling of regret to build as a motivator to change.

EXERCISE 4A – PRETENTIOUS, HANGING ON

You regret pretending and are willing to change. You are at Level 4 if you regret pretending and are ready to change. Change can be tough if you have been pretending for a long time. You must be willing to let go of all you have achieved with this failed strategy and to start over on a more solid foundation. Change might not be easy, but it is absolutely necessary. We want you to feed your motivation to change.

TASK: Write down how your life would be better if you had never pretended or taken credit for the accomplishments of others. What might you have achieved? For what might you be proud? What skills might you have gained?

SESSION 2

EXERCISE 1B – PRETENTIOUS, HANGING ON

Undeserved opportunities. Hopefully, you have become a little bit more aware that pretending has been a big issue in your life that you need to face. Session 2 will ask you to identify specific areas where you may have been pretending or taking credit that you don't deserve. You can't change what you can't see. Please be open and honest with yourself. This might not be fun, but it is important. Today we want you to focus on any and all opportunities you have gained by pretending to be who you aren't or by lying. You may have exaggerated on your résumé to get a job. Or you might have pretended to be more successful than you are in order to win the love of someone in your life. You might have lied about your experience in order to be seen as more qualified than you were.

TASK: Review your whole life and write down everything that comes to mind. Review your list every day for the next week and add to it.

EXERCISE 2B – PRETENTIOUS, HANGING ON

Undeserved success on the back of someone else or due to luck. Now we want you to focus on successes that you took credit for when you knew they were due to the work of someone else or the result of luck. You may have cheated on a test, borrowing the answers from a friend. Or you may have taken credit for someone's project or report at work, pretending you did the work when someone who worked for you actually did all of the work. You know you don't deserve credit for these things. You might also have been in the right place at the right time but people think you created the positive outcome. You didn't correct them.

TASK: Make a list of all of the successes you took credit for that you didn't deserve. Revisit this list every day for the next week and add to it.

EXERCISE 3B – PRETENTIOUS, HANGING ON

Undeserved reputation: Bernie Madoff. Now we are asking you to think about your reputation—how people think of you. Perhaps people think you are courageous when, in fact, you aren't at all. Or, they might think you are wise when you just repeat the things you have heard without truly understanding what they're saying. You might have a reputation for being popular when that is only a façade you have created.

TASK: Make a list of the misunderstandings people have about your character. What do they believe that you know isn't true? You have pretended to be what you are not and allowed others to believe the lie. Review this list every day for the next week and add to it.

EXERCISE 4B – PRETENTIOUS, HANGING ON

Undeserved love. Finally, where do you accept love and acceptance where you know you don't deserve it? Perhaps you talk negatively about your best friend behind her back but to her face you are nice. She likes you only because she doesn't know the truth. Or you may have cheated on your spouse and not admitted to your unfaithfulness. You think you got away clean because he still loves you, but you know he would feel differently if he knew the truth.

TASK: Make a list of all of the relationships you have where you know people would think of you differently if they knew the truth about what you think, what you have said, and what you have done. Take your time. Revisit this list every day for the next week and add to it.

SESSION 3

EXERCISE 1C – PRETENTIOUS, HANGING ON

In Session 3 we want you to carefully identify the people in your life to which you are pretending. In Session 2 you should have identified some areas in your life where pretending has hurt you. Pretending is always damaging to the people in your life. They believed in you based on false information. Their trust in you has been seriously damaged. Let's start with work/school.

TASK: Make a list of all of the people at work/school who believe in you based on your lies and pretense. Take your time and review the list every day for the next week, adding names. As you review this list, consider how these people would think of you if they knew the whole truth.

EXERCISE 2C – PRETENTIOUS, HANGING ON

We may have covered this relationship in Session 2, but it is worth visiting again. Partnership and marriage are built on trust. Trust is built on truth. The more deceitful you have been, the more you reduce the possibility of intimacy, which is the glue of any good marriage.

TASK: Make a list of all of the secrets you are keeping from your partner/spouse and all of the lies you have been telling him/her. Add to this list through the week. Ask yourself why you are keeping secrets and telling lies. What are you hoping to get or protect?

EXERCISE 3C – PRETENTIOUS, HANGING ON

If you have children, what have you been pretending in your relationship with them? You may be pretending you were better at sports than you were and so putting them under undo pressure to live up to a reputation you never had. The same could be true of grades in school. You might be telling them stories about your accomplishments that are embellished and are told only to make you look good. The desire to look good in front of your children is natural, but to do so under false pretenses undermines their true respect.

TASK: Make a list of all of the lies you have told or are telling your children. Now write down all of the things you are pretending to be, or to have done, that are not true.

EXERCISE 4C – PRETENTIOUS, HANGING ON

Finally, consider your friendships. People like you, admire you, and want to be around you. To what extend is their friendship with you built on lies and deceit? Only you will know. But friendship built on deceit will eventually fall apart as your lies become apparent. You will fall from being a friend to being someone with whom no one wants to speak. You will lose whatever respect you were receiving.

TASK: Think through all of your friendships. List the ones that are built on the wrong foundation. Add to this list every day for the next week.

SESSION 4

EXERCISE 1D – PRETENTIOUS, HANGING ON

Feeling of being a fake. Session 4 will help you to become more aware of how your pretending has impacted you internally. It is likely that this pattern of thinking and behaving has been so much a part of your life that it has become second nature and you have become deadened to its negative impact on your life. Let's get started by asking you to notice how it feels to know you are pretending to be who you are not. Can you get in touch with the moment you decided to lie about yourself and your accomplishments? Can you see in retrospect that you were making the wrong choice? You may have seen that it might give you something in the moment but knew in your heart that it couldn't be sustained.

TASK: Write down six instances where you pretended. Each day for the next week, take one and review it in your mind. Practice going to the decision point and feeling the impact of your choice to pretend.

EXERCISE 2D – PRETENTIOUS, HANGING ON

Fear of being discovered. Next, we want you to face the anxiety you created by pretending. As soon as you chose to lie about yourself, you created the anxiety of being discovered. You had to cover your tracks. You had to avoid certain conversations. You may have had to avoid certain people who knew the truth about your life. You worried when the phone rang that this call would be the one that exposed you as a pretender.

TASK: Make a list of all of the worry and anxiety you have created by pretending. Each day for the next week add to it.

EXERCISE 3D – PRETENTIOUS, HANGING ON

Gradual loss of knowing oneself. Even more subtle may be the gradual loss of knowing yourself that you created by your pretense. The more you pretended, the less you became aware of the truth about you. Over time, you believed your own lies and sold out more and more of your own uniqueness.

TASK: Go back to your list from Exercise 1. Review those times you pretended but imagine you had chosen not to pretend. What might you have learned on that road? Write down whatever comes to mind.

EXERCISE 4D – PRETENTIOUS, HANGING ON

No foundation for your own power. Finally, your life of pretending has greatly inhibited your ability to create a useful and powerful life. Very little of your reputation, success, and possessions are due to your own ability and character. You have built your life on a foundation of deceit and pretense rather than on something substantial and durable. What would it be like to start over? You would need to give up all of that which you have been pretending and to go back to whatever little bit you know about yourself. That might seem like a radical thing to do, but it is the only way to recover your life.

TASK: Make a list of whatever you know to be true about you and your abilities. Be honest but also be kind to yourself. You are coming home.

FACTOR – PRETENTIOUS

Give up pretending to be who you aren't and whatever success you have by pretending in order to find your true source of strength and power.

SELF-ASSESSED RATING - ERODING

Much of your life is built on pretending to be who you are not and taking credit for things you did not earn. However you do have glimpses of who you truly are.

SESSION 1

EXERCISE 1A – PRETENTIOUS, ERODING

Your life is eroding because you have been substantially pretending to be who you are not in one or more areas of your life. Such a pattern is not sustainable and will eventually always lead to embarrassment, loss, and shame. The purpose of Session 1 is to review the major areas of your life so you can identify those places where pretending is undermining your success and well-being. Let's get started.

In Session 1 we are asking you to review your work/school history.

TASK: List all of your achievements that have been gained by pretending to be who you are not, stealing the work of someone else, or lying about what you actually knew or did. Be thorough. Review your list each day for the next week and add content.

EXERCISE 2A – PRETENTIOUS, ERODING

Now review your home life. Where have you been pretending with the people in your family? Perhaps you have been keeping secrets from your spouse. Or you are lying to your parents. Or you may be pretending with your children by taking credit for accomplishments in the past you did not earn. By pretending, you are setting up all of these important relationships for a crisis in trust when the truth you have been concealing comes to light.

TASK: Make a list of all of the places you are pretending with family members. Review it each day for the following week and add to it.

EXERCISE 3A – PRETENTIOUS, ERODING

Your integrity. Next, consider all of the lies you try to believe about yourself. You are sacrificing your integrity every day by falsifying how you portray yourself to the world. It is so important that you come to grips with every lapse in your integrity. What do you say that you don't mean? What do you not say because you don't want the truth to be exposed? What do you pretend to be that you know isn't true?

TASK: List all lapses in integrity that you can think of.

EXERCISE 4A – PRETENTIOUS, ERODING

Your confidence. One of the unintended consequences of pretending is to undermine your confidence in yourself. Since you know you have not been honest and so have acquired whatever success you have under false pretenses, you have betrayed your faith in your own capabilities. You have trusted a lie over the truth about yourself. It is so important for you to increase your awareness of how you have been hurting yourself with your pretending.

TASK: Fill in the blanks of this sentence in as many different ways as you can. "By pretending to be/do _______, I have undermined my confidence that I am competent to _______." Revisit this exercise every day for the next week and add content.

SESSION 2

EXERCISE 1B – PRETENTIOUS, ERODING

The journey away from pretending and toward independence requires you to close your integrity gaps wherever they exist. In essence, you must admit to those whom you have been fooling that you were pretending and don't deserve the trust, respect, raise, loan, etc. that they have extended to you. We know this is a lot to ask. It is difficult to give up the façade you have created and to admit the truth about who you truly are. But this is the first step of change. Let's start with work.

TASK: Make a list of the people to whom you need to speak. Who believes something that is not true about you? To whom have you been lying? Whom have you cheated? Take this week to meet with everyone on your list, admitting the truth to each one.

EXERCISE 2B – PRETENTIOUS, ERODING

Now, let's focus on your relationship with your spouse/partner. This is the most important relationship in your life, because it is your best opportunity to cultivate a truly intimate connection with another human being. It is your chance to truly know and be known by another person. To the extent you have been pretending, lying, or keeping secrets, you have been cutting yourself off from the very opportunity this relationship is meant to be. So, make a list of everything that you need to share with your partner. What you had for lunch yesterday isn't necessary to share. But everything you are afraid to share or ashamed of is something that needs to be on your list.

TASK: Sit down with your partner sometime this week, apologize, and have the hard conversation of coming clean.

EXERCISE 3B – PRETENTIOUS, ERODING

If you have children, you may have been pretending with them. You may have pretended to have been better at sports than you were. Or you might be pretending to have gotten better grades when you were their ages. You may be using your pretending to earn their respect or to put pressure on them to be like you. The reason doesn't really matter. Whatever respect they have for you based on your pretending is a sham and sets them up for great disappointment when they finally discover the truth. It is far better for you to earn their respect by being honest than for them to learn the truth about you from someone else.

TASK: Make a list of all of the lies and pretense you have with your children. This week have conversations with each of them and tell them the truth.

EXERCISE 4B – PRETENTIOUS, ERODING

Finally, consider all of the ways you have been pretending with your friends. Friends are important because these people are potential allies in your life. They are people with resources and opportunities on whom you can call for assistance when you need help. They are also people who may, from time to time, need your help. These relationships should be built on trust and mutual respect. To the extent you have been pretending, your friendships are built on a weak foundation and are liable to collapse at any time.

TASK: Make a list of how you have pretended or lied to your friends. Think through relationships from your past and friendships you have lost due to your pretending. Use the next week to schedule time with everyone on your list. Apologize, ask for forgiveness, and admit to whatever you have been pretending and to all of your lies.

SESSION 3

EXERCISE 1C – PRETENTIOUS, ERODING

Giving back what isn't yours. The next step in giving up pretending is to give back whatever was gotten under false pretenses. Holding on to that which you don't deserve will continue to erode your self-esteem and confidence. It will undermine your integrity and weaken your ability to build a solid life. Let's get started.

In this session we are asking you to give back to others whatever material things you have that you did not honestly earn.

TASK: Take your time and make a complete list. You may have guilted a family member into buying you a car or loaning you money that you never intended to repay by pretending to be in greater need than was the complete truth. Once you have made a complete list, begin planning for how and when you will return those things to the people who gave them to you.

EXERCISE 2C – PRETENTIOUS, ERODING

Giving up what you don't deserve. The second step in giving back what isn't yours is surrendering any praise, admiration, position, or privilege you may have received by pretending. You may have gotten an award you didn't deserve. Perhaps your boss promoted you because of work someone else had done and of which she was unaware. Perhaps your spouse is giving you love that, if they knew your secrets, would be retracted.

TASK: Make a complete list and then set up meetings with each person and surrender what you don't deserve. We know this is difficult to do. But it is like pruning a tree. You cut off some branches so that the tree will be stronger and will produce more fruit.

EXERCISE 3C – PRETENTIOUS, ERODING

Being honest where you have been deceitful. Now we want you to face any and all lies you have told. Perhaps you have told lies that didn't really get you anything or anywhere. Regardless, every lie makes it more difficult for you and the world around you to see your true value. You have been pretending to be who you aren't and so missing the truth about who you really are.

TASK: Make a list of every lie you have told and why you told it. What were you hiding? What were you hoping to gain? Reread your list every day for the next week and determine that you will speak only truthfully from this point on.

EXERCISE 4C – PRETENTIOUS, ERODING

Honoring yourself. These exercises have been challenging and difficult. We have asked you to do things that you have never done before. We have asked you to give up habits you have had your whole life. We have asked you to do things that caused you pain, embarrassment, and loss. And, you have done it...because you knew everything we asked, while difficult, was good for you. It was the right advice. It pointed you in the right direction. What is that direction? It is the direction of who you truly are. It is our belief that you have greatness in you. It is because you have greatness that you should never pretend to be who you are not. It is far better for you to cultivate who you are. It is only on this path that you will discover and expand your greatness.

TASK: Make a list of wherever you have seen even a glimmer of your greatness. It may be in an act of kindness toward a stranger. Or, it may be in a deep feeling of commitment to your child or partner. You may have been courageous at work one day. This list points to who you really are. Reread it every day this week and allow the goodness of those choices to fill you up with pride to be who you are.

SESSION 4

EXERCISE 1D – PRETENTIOUS, ERODING

Where did you start pretending? This session will ask you to go back to the beginning of your pretending in order to start over on a new course that will make your life much stronger. We want you to think back to where you started to pretend. Think back to your childhood. Do you remember the event where you knew the truth would not get you what you wanted or would cause some sort of difficulty for you? You faced a critical decision and you chose the wrong path. It was easy to do because in that moment you lacked the confidence in yourself or the courage to make the best decision. But, it started you down the road that undermined the strength of your life. Consider the cost of your bad choice that day.

TASK: Write down all that you have lost because you went down the wrong road.

EXERCISE 2D – PRETENTIOUS, ERODING

What would you have done if you hadn't pretended? Now, go back to the day you chose to pretend. Imagine that you had made the other choice. You chose to be honest. The immediate result may have been that you would not have gotten something that you wanted or may have gotten into some sort of trouble. But, once you had gotten past that situation, you would still be connected to your integrity. If you chose the road of being honest, how would your life have evolved? What do you imagine you would have done that you didn't do? What do you imagine you would have become?

TASK: Form a picture of who you might have been if you hadn't pretended. This is the picture of the life you are getting ready to create.

EXERCISE 3D – PRETENTIOUS, ERODING

Are you willing to do that now? We all have some natural instincts that are powerful and useful guides. The picture you painted of your potential life in Exercise 2 is probably a good roadmap for the life you were meant to build. How would you start to build that now? What is the very first thing you would need to do to begin to move down the road toward the life you were meant to have?

TASK: Write it down. Now look at it carefully. Is it about pretending or about being your truthful self? If there is any pretending, go back and change it. Make sure your first step is a truthful expression of your thoughts, abilities, character, and skills.

EXERCISE 4D – PRETENTIOUS, ERODING

Staying on course. We want to leave you with the responsibility to be vigilant about your integrity. You have been in the habit of pretending for a long time. You have now started a new habit: one of being open, honest, and clear. In order to strengthen your new habit, you need to do two things. First, be on guard about the tendency to lie and pretend to get what you want. You might find your first inclination is to pretend.

TASK: Learn to catch yourself quickly and to change course. If you find you actually have pretended, go back and correct it as soon as you discover it. Second, notice the benefit you are receiving by being honest. It should become obvious to you that you have less anxiety because you have nothing to hide. You feel more secure because you are actually earning the things you receive. Stay on the right road.

FACTOR – PRETENTIOUS

Give up pretending to be who you aren't and whatever success you have by pretending in order to find your true source of strength and power.

SELF-ASSESSED RATING - TREADING WATER

You are honest about yourself much of the time but occasionally pretend because you think it is necessary to do so to get ahead or keep the peace.

SESSION 1

EXERCISE 1A – PRETENTIOUS, TREADING WATER

You are treading water because you have been pretending in some aspects of your life. Pretending is limiting your ability to move forward and to grow. Session 1 is designed to assist you in assessing where you are being your honest self and where you are pretending. Until you can identify your pretense, it is almost impossible to give it up. You may have been pretending so long that you almost believe your pretense is true. Let's get started.

Consider any and all ways you may have been pretending at work. You may cut corners that you conceal. You may pretend to be smarter or more knowledgeable than you are. You may borrow the work of others. You may have embellished your résumé to get your job. Be completely honest with yourself.

TASK: Review your list every day for the next week and add to it any insights you gain.

EXERCISE 2A – PRETENTIOUS, TREADING WATER

Now, consider any pretending you have been doing with your spouse/partner. You may be pretending to be happier with that person than you actually are. You may have secrets—some you consider too small to mention. But they are secrets nevertheless. You might have some habits that you hide or make choices that you don't want to talk about. Every time you conceal something or pretend something you weaken your ability to expand your intimacy into something vibrant and growing.

TASK: Make a list of all that comes to mind. Review that list every day for the next week and add whatever comes to mind.

EXERCISE 3A – PRETENTIOUS, TREADING WATER

If you have children, consider any ways you have been pretending with them. Your children look up to you and naturally want to respect you. To the extent their respect and affection is based on deceit you are setting them up for disillusionment and mistrust. It is far better that you come clean with them than to wait for them to discover your pretense on their own. You may be pretending to be more successful than you are or to have accomplished more in your life than you have. Parents can easily exaggerate their strengths and underrepresent their weaknesses and failures.

TASK: Make an honest assessment of where you have been pretending. Review it every day for the next week and add content.

EXERCISE 4A – PRETENTIOUS, TREADING WATER

Finally, consider where you have been pretending with friends, neighbors, and associates. You have wanted to look good, to be liked, to be accepted and respected, and so you dressed yourself up. You may have told stories that weren't exactly true. You may have spent more than you could afford on a house or car in order to portray yourself as more successful than you are. While you may have enjoyed the admiration of your friends, you did not understand that you were weakening yourself. You were creating a façade that masked your true self.

TASK: Make a list of all of your pretending with your friends, neighbors, and associates. Review it every day for the next week and add any insights you have.

SESSION 2

EXERCISE 1B – PRETENTIOUS, TREADING WATER

What do you want? Pretending is always driven by one of three motivations. Today we ask you to consider what you hoped to get from pleasing. It is only when we come across something we want that we choose how we will attempt to secure it. It could be a possession, an honor, acceptance, love, approval, or almost anything. The choice before us is always the same. Do we try to get it by being honest, being ourselves, and doing our best? Or do we try to get it by lying, pretending, and hiding?

TASK: Please take some time to review your life and list all of the things you have tried to acquire by pretending to be who you were not. You gained these things under false pretenses; hence you created for yourself some insecurity as to how much you deserve to have and to keep them. Review your list every day and add to it any insights you gain.

EXERCISE 2B – PRETENTIOUS, TREADING WATER

What do you fear? The second motivation to pretend is to avoid something you fear. Sometimes we encounter situations that are difficult and that we want to avoid. You did something wrong and got caught. Something didn't get done that should have been done, and you don't want to be discovered. You aren't what someone wants you to be, and you might lose their affection or respect if they know the truth. In such cases, you have the same choice. You can tell the truth about yourself and accept the consequences, or you can pretend to be who you are not in the hope you can avoid a negative outcome. Perhaps you lied to your teacher because you didn't do your homework. Or you cheated on a test because you hadn't studied. By making this choice, you voted against yourself. You chose to consider yourself not good enough for your life. You pretended to be someone else.

TASK: Please make a list of all of the consequences you hoped to avoid by pretending throughout your life. Review your list every day this week and add any insights you gain.

EXERCISE 3B – PRETENTIOUS, TREADING WATER

What are you trying to control? The third motivation to pretend is to try to control something that you want to occur. It is easy for everyone to become attached to certain outcomes that we want to secure. You may want to stay married and not get divorced. You might want to remain employed and not be laid off. You might want to remain included in your social network and not be rejected. When you envision those negative outcomes, they feel terrible, as if your life would fall apart. So you begin to try to manage your circumstances by pretending. If only you appear to be what your spouse, boss, or friends want you to be, you can keep things as they are. The problem is that life is not meant to be managed. The challenges of life are meant to be faced honestly and courageously. When we try to manage them by pretending, we are only putting off the inevitable and undermining our courage and growth.

TASK: Make a list of all that you have and are trying to control by pretending. Revisit your list every day for the next week and add any insights you have.

EXERCISE 4B – PRETENTIOUS, TREADING WATER

Letting go. Now, it is time to let go of all that you have wanted, all that you have feared, and all that you have tried to control. This is a big step. Go through your lists for the last three sessions and imagine what it would be like if you let everything on your lists go. You give up wanting what you wanted. You give up fearing that which you have been avoiding. You give up managing that which you have been controlling. You invite life to bring to you whatever challenges it wants. You will face them honestly and openly. You will do your best and make that good enough. You will be committed to being yourself more than to anything else. You will always vote for your honor and integrity above anything else.

TASK: Every day this week choose to vote for your honor and integrity.

SESSION 3

EXERCISE 1C – PRETENTIOUS, TREADING WATER

Accepting yourself for who you are. Giving up pretending requires you to accept yourself for who you are. While it is certainly true that you aren't good at everything and it may be true that you aren't everything the people in your life want you to be, it is critical that you accept yourself for who you are. It is interesting that we often want from others what we aren't willing to give ourselves. We want acceptance, affirmation, and praise from the world, but aren't giving those things to ourselves. Pretending to be who we aren't is the exact opposite of self-acceptance. You must accept yourself for all that you are—the strong and the weak, the good and the bad.

TASK: Make a list of all of your strengths and weaknesses. Review the list every day for the next week. Add to it and offer yourself acceptance for all that you wrote down.

EXERCISE 2C – PRETENTIOUS, TREADING WATER

Knowing you are enough. Self-acceptance is the first step in giving up pretending. The second step is knowing that you are enough for all that you need and want in life. In some ways this is a bit of a faith commitment we are asking you to make. But it is very important. You must believe that being who you are is much better than pretending to be someone you are not. The more you believe that you are enough, the more you will step into your life challenges with confidence and, in doing so, will gain new skills, confidence, and courage.

TASK: This week we want you to practice a mantra, something you will repeat to yourself at least three times each day. Say, "I am enough to have whatever I want." The more you say it, the more you will come to believe it and the more it will show itself to be true.

EXERCISE 3C – PRETENTIOUS, TREADING WATER

Cultivating your integrity. Perhaps your most important attribute is your character. This might not always seem to be true. But your character is like the operating system of your computer. Everything that happens on the screen is controlled by the operating system. In the same way, everything that comes out of your mouth, all of the choices you make, every attitude, and every belief extends from your character. Hence, having strong character makes you strong. Character is strengthened by our integrity. Integrity means being whole. When we say one thing and do another, we weaken our character. When we say exactly what we think, our integrity grows. Be on the lookout every day this week for the choices you make and choose to make ones that build your integrity and so strengthen your character.

TASK: Keep a list of all of your successes.

EXERCISE 4C – PRETENTIOUS, TREADING WATER

Honoring yourself. Finally, make yourself important. When you pretend, you are making others big and making yourself small. You are acting as if they have things that you need and that you must please them if you are going to get what you want. Instead of seeing yourself in such a small way, act as a king/queen among kings/queens. You are not needy in any way. In fact, you are rich. You certainly are rich in character, integrity, and dignity. Carry yourself with self-respect. Interact with others as someone who is rich and noble. Instead of focusing on what you need from others, shift your focus on what you can give others. The more you carry yourself with greatness, the more the world will honor you.

TASK: Practice every day carrying yourself as someone of great character.

SESSION 4

EXERCISE 1D – PRETENTIOUS, TREADING WATER

Correcting misunderstanding. In this session we want to assist you in cleaning out any old baggage that may be limiting your ability to step out of all pretending. Let's get started. Today we want you to focus on any misunderstanding people have toward you that needs to be corrected. The people in your life may see you as more (or less) than is true about you. They may think you are better, smarter, and more courageous and determined than you know is true of you. Or they might think you are less trustworthy, caring, or giving than you know to be the case.

TASK: Make a list of any misunderstandings others have toward you of which you are aware. Use this week to go to each person on your list and correct their misunderstanding.

EXERCISE 2D – PRETENTIOUS, TREADING WATER

Admitting to deceit. Next, we want you to review any place in your life where you are lying or deceiving others and come clean. Until you do, you won't be whole. Your integrity will be weak. You will have difficulty expanding your life and making it stronger.

TASK: Make a complete list and then summon your courage and have the difficult conversations. Start by telling the person that you have not been telling the truth. Apologize. Tell them what is true. Ask for their forgiveness. Promise not to deceive them in the future.

EXERCISE 3D – PRETENTIOUS, TREADING WATER

Giving to others what is theirs. Now we want you to consider anything you possess that you received through pretending. Make a list. This list should include possessions, but also honors, relationships, and care and acceptance that you don't deserve. You have pretended to be in greater need than you were and others rescued you. You may have pretended to be faithful when you weren't. Again, this is not easy to do.

TASK: When your list is complete, we want you to give back whatever you gained by pretense. Go back to each person; tell them that you were pretending to be who you weren't and that you want to return what they gave to you. You won't believe how much stronger you will be for having done so.

EXERCISE 4D – PRETENTIOUS, TREADING WATER

Being honest in all that you say. Now we want to encourage you to keep moving forward in building a stronger life. The most important thing you can do is to be completely honest in every word you speak. This is something to practice. Notice if you are considering saying something that isn't true.

TASK: Catch yourself and speak truthfully. Notice if you said something that wasn't true. Go back and correct it. Notice if you aren't saying everything you have to say. Say whatever you are withholding. Practicing complete candor is the very best way to move forward out of all pretending. Good luck.

FACTOR – PRETENTIOUS

Giving up pretending to be who you aren't and whatever success you have by pretending in order to find your true source of strength and power.

SELF-ASSESSED RATING - GROWING

You hardly ever pretend to be who you are not except in one or two situations in which you don't know how to be yourself.

SESSION 1

EXERCISE 1A – PRETENTIOUS, GROWING

How much are you dishonest and why? You are growing but not fully thriving because there is some issue involving pretending that is holding you back. Session 1 is designed to help you assess where you might be getting in your own way. The good news is that you have largely freed yourself from pretense and so know what it is like to be and express your true self. The bad news is that, for some reason, you have maintained some dependence on pretending. Let's get started.

In Exercise 1 we are asking you to focus on relationships where you aren't fully honest. You are holding back in some way. Or, you are pretending something that isn't true for you. You may be acting more loyal than you feel. Or, you might be pretending to be accepting when you have judgments.

TASK: Notice where you are pretending. It should be focused on only a very few relationships or situations.

EXERCISE 2A – PRETENTIOUS, GROWING

How often do you take credit for something you don't deserve and why? A second place where you might be pretending is by taking credit for something you know you don't deserve. Your boss may think you won a major deal when you know you had nothing to do with it. Or, you may act like your possessions are your own when someone else paid for them. These can be subtle distinctions but they are important. Wherever you are pretending to take credit when you don't deserve it, you are undermining your own integrity.

TASK: Make a list of anything you are taking credit for that you don't deserve. Review your list every day for the next week and add any insights you gain.

EXERCISE 3A – PRETENTIOUS, GROWING

How much do you pretend and why? Next, focus your attention on anything you are pretending to be. You might be pretending to know things you don't know or pretending to be confident when you are frightened. You might be pretending to like someone more than you do. It isn't likely that you are doing a lot of pretending, which makes it even more important to wonder why you would maintain such a negative behavior anywhere. But, it is in such things that you limit your ability to thrive.

TASK: List everything you are pretending to be. Ask yourself why you are pretending.

EXERCISE 4A – PRETENTIOUS, GROWING

How much do you withhold and why? Finally, ask yourself what you might be withholding. You may be truthful for the most part but holding back something that you think might upset or disrupt someone in your life. You may have some small secret that you have been keeping. You might not have told your boss about mistakes you have made. Even small withholds damage your ability to be fully free and open. They leave you open to anxiety about being discovered.

TASK: Make a list of anything you have been withholding. Review your list every day this week and add content. Ask yourself why you have been withholding this.

SESSION 2

EXERCISE 1B – PRETENTIOUS, GROWING

Giving up all lying. The remaining sessions are designed to provide you with the skills necessary to give up and remain without pretending. You may have mastered some of these skills or you may find that you have some things to learn from each of them. Session 2 will focus on candor. Candor has three aspects. The first is telling your truth. This seems so simple on the surface. No one knows THE truth. But everyone knows his/her truth. Your truth is simply what you think things to be. It isn't modified by what others want or don't want to hear. It doesn't change because of the consequences. It is your truth. Learning to tell your truth all of the time is a powerful way to confront any pretending.

TASK: We want you to practice telling your truth in every encounter you have this week. Keep a diary. Notice when you were enticed to modify your truth and why. See if you can speak your truth all of the time.

EXERCISE 2B – PRETENTIOUS, GROWING

Saying everything you know. The second aspect of candor is saying everything you know. It is possible to speak your truth while withholding certain information or thoughts. You are not lying, but you know you are avoiding saying everything. Now, we should be clear, by everything we don't mean everything that is in your mind. We are talking about things you know are relevant to the conversation and that you are choosing to withhold to gain some end. It may be to protect someone's feelings or to create some outcome. Regardless, you know you aren't being fully candid.

TASK: This week we want you to stretch yourself and to pay attention to any times you are withholding something that should be said. Again, use your diary. Notice what you were tempted to withhold and the reason. See if you cannot withhold anything the entire week.

EXERCISE 3B – PRETENTIOUS, GROWING

Knowing everything there is to know. The third aspect of candor is knowing all there is to know. Even if you don't lie and withhold, you can choose not to know information that you could or should know but have been avoiding. You might not want to know the time because you are planning to be late. When you are asked about why you were late, you can truthfully say that you didn't know the time. You are choosing to avoid being responsible and accountable. Or, you can deliberately not pay attention to how much your spouse is drinking at night because you know he will be angry if you talk to him about drinking too much.

TASK: This week ask yourself if there are things you are choosing not to know, things you are avoiding because of the possible consequences of knowing. Write down everything that comes to mind as you review this exercise every day. You may be surprised by all that you discover. We are asking you to open your eyes and your mind to know everything that you should know so that you can step into full candor and openness in your life.

EXERCISE 4B – PRETENTIOUS, GROWING

Acknowledging negative energy. In this session we are asking you to notice if you have any negative energy toward anyone in your life. Negative energy is the result of slights, insults, mistreatment, or offense in the past or present. As a result, you have some resentment toward these people. Maintaining negative energy is a great temptation to pretend. It is so easy to act like you are okay when you are around these people while inwardly you are angry or scared.

TASK: In order to get free of your pretending, please make a list of everyone with whom you have negative energy. Revisit your list every day this week and add names as you become aware of them.

SESSION 3

EXERCISE 1C – PRETENTIOUS, GROWING

Your goal in this session is to "get clean" with everyone toward whom you have unresolved negative energy. Sometimes this can be done simply by clarifying a misunderstanding. We often don't know the reason why people have done the things that have hurt us. Perhaps it was unintentional or something got in their way. You may have been told that your best friend criticized you behind your back, but, in truth, she wasn't critical at all. You won't know until you reach out to each person on your list and admit to them that you have harbored negative feelings that you want to release.

TASK: Tell them the story you have in your mind about what you think they did and why you think they did it. See if your conversation clears up your misunderstanding.

EXERCISE 2C – PRETENTIOUS, GROWING

In this session, we will discuss how to "get clean" when the issue isn't a misunderstanding. Sometimes, the people in your life acted with malice and ill will toward you. Their intention was to harm you in some way. How do you deal with the wounds others have purposefully inflicted on you? Sometimes you must simply forgive. Forgiveness means canceling a debt owed you. You might have been wronged, but carrying the hurt is now hurting you. Nursing those old wounds is limiting your ability to embrace the fullness in your life. It is time to give it up.

TASK: Take the next week to clean up all of the relationships where you need to forgive. Forgiveness is more about your own heart than it is about the other person. You may choose to tell them that you have forgiven them or not. Most importantly, you will release yourself.

EXERCISE 3C – PRETENTIOUS, GROWING

Assessing where you may not be whole. The best part of giving up pretending is that it allows you to be whole. It takes energy to pretend to be who you are not. You have to remember to keep up your pretense and must conceal the truth about yourself. Giving up pretending allows you to be yourself, speak your mind, and act according to your attitudes and beliefs.

TASK: This week we want you to scan your life for any places where you might not yet be completely free. It doesn't have to be something big. Just notice and keep a running list of any conversations or decisions where you had second thoughts or found yourself holding back in any way. Notice the strength you feel when you are whole and the weakness you introduce when you pretend even in some small way. The more you notice the difference, the more you will be naturally motivated to guard your wholeness and refuse to sacrifice it for anything or anyone.

EXERCISE 4C – PRETENTIOUS, GROWING

Keeping integrity before everything else. Being vs. doing. Many people seem to act as if the success in their lives is about what they do. They are successful if they get a good job, make a lot of money, have a lot of power. We are convinced that real success in life has more to do with who you are than with what you do. We say that your "being" is far more important than your "doing." Weak people can create outward success but often struggle to maintain it. Strong people build a foundation upon which a successful future can be built.

TASK: We want you to focus on your "being" this week. Notice your character. Act with honor. Speak candidly. Notice how people treat you when you carry yourself in such a way. You will earn a respect that is well deserved. This is encouragement to carry yourself with such dignity every day for the rest of your life.

SESSION 4

EXERCISE 1D – PRETENTIOUS, GROWING

This last session focuses on how you can most powerfully relate to others without pretending. It is about the power of your word. Not that long ago, there was little need for lawyers because people made agreements with a handshake. Basically, they gave their word and it wasn't taken lightly. People lived by their word regardless of the circumstances. We call this being impeccable in your word. When you do what you say you will do 100 percent of the time, people find you to be dependable, trustworthy, and of good character. They like dealing with you and relating to you.

TASK: We invite you to look at your life and see where you aren't currently being impeccable in your word. It might be in big or little ways. Perhaps you say you will be home at 7:00 but come in at 7:30. It is only 30 minutes so it may not seem like a big deal to you. But your child may have been waiting for you since 7:00 to share something very important and has been disappointed by your absence. We want you to set a very high bar for yourself and will teach you the skills to keep it.

EXERCISE 2D – PRETENTIOUS, GROWING

Saying no. The first skill in being impeccable in your agreements is learning to say no. When you make agreements to appease others, when you overcommit to things, when you don't think through your interest in the agreement you are making, you are likely to set yourself up to not follow through. How many items have been lingering on your "to-do" list for months, or even years? Start by learning to say no. Say no to whatever you don't want to do. Say no to whatever you know you won't be able to do. Say no a lot. Sometimes your boss may ask you to agree to a deadline you know is unrealistic. You probably shouldn't just say no. But you can explain all that is on your plate and all you have committed to do. Ask if the boss wants to reorder your commitments or will accept a more realistic deadline.

TASK: This week practice saying no. Notice when it is easy and when it is not. Learn to say no even when it is not easy.

EXERCISE 3D – PRETENTIOUS, GROWING

Making clear agreements. Next, we want you to learn to make clear agreements. Clear agreements have a well-defined deliverable and a specific date and time when they will be completed. When you don't make clear agreements, you leave room for misunderstanding. You might agree to get a report to your boss next week. He might think you meant Monday while you really were thinking of Friday. On Tuesday he is angry because you missed his deadline even while you think you still have a few more days. Or, you agreed to get him the sales report but weren't specific as to what would be included. Clear agreements leave no room for misunderstanding.

TASK: This week focus on making very clear agreements with specific deliverables, dates, and times. Keep a record of all of the agreements you make.

EXERCISE 4D – PRETENTIOUS, GROWING

Dealing w/ broken agreements. Regardless of your efforts and good intentions, occasionally you will fail to be impeccable. Sometimes, it will be for no fault of yours. You might get a flat tire on the way to a meeting. Or your son might need to go to the emergency room. When you know you won't be able to keep your agreement, immediately call the person with whom you have it and renegotiate it. When you do so, you maintain trust in the relationship. At other times, you may have simply forgotten about your agreement. When that occurs, it is critical that you go to the person with whom you had the agreement and admit that you broke it.

TASK: Apologize and ask for forgiveness. Admit that you broke trust and that you want to restore trust.

EXERCISE SERIES: PERSONAL COMMITMENT

FACTOR – PERSONAL COMMITMENT

The capacity to voluntarily choose your goals, properly manage your behaviors, and discipline yourself to follow through on your plan.

SELF-ASSESSED RATING - HANGING ON

You either don't make commitments, or rarely, if ever, keep the ones you make. You rarely set goals for yourself, and if you do, you don't have the discipline to follow through on achieving them.

SESSION 1

EXERCISE 1A – PERSONAL COMMITMENT, HANGING ON

Session 1 is designed to help you honestly face the current state of your life and, rather than making excuses, to come to grip with some of the reasons for your situation. You are hanging on by your fingernails because your life lacks order, direction, and/or the discipline necessary to act in your own best interest. Let's get started.

TASK: Make a list of your greatest problems and concerns. Don't hold back. This is your opportunity to complain without restraint. Review your list and add to it every day for the next week.

EXERCISE 2A – PERSONAL COMMITMENT, HANGING ON

This week, we want you to shift your focus to all that you want but don't have. Again, don't hold back. You are free to add anything to this list, but try to be honest with yourself. There is nothing wrong with wanting things. In fact, our wants and wishes often provide the necessary motivation to make constructive changes. Giving up on wanting is only further evidence that your life is out of control.

TASK: Write down everything that comes to mind and add to it every day for the next week.

EXERCISE 3A – PERSONAL COMMITMENT, HANGING ON

We expect your lists from the last two weeks to be quite long. There are many problems and concerns. There are many things you want that you don't have.

TASK: We now want you to review both lists and to ask yourself how you expect your situation to get better. How are you expecting your concerns and problems to lessen? How are you hoping to get the things you want? It may be difficult to answer these questions. If so, notice that you simply don't think about such things. It is almost as if you are hoping life will turn out good for you without putting any thought into how you might shape your life. You are wishing rather than planning. There is nothing wrong with wishing. But wishing is rarely enough in itself.

EXERCISE 4A – PERSONAL COMMITMENT, HANGING ON

It is easy to imagine that other people ought to be the ones to solve your problems or to give you what you want. You may actually have a list of people you are expecting to show up and help out, but you might notice that your life isn't at all what you want it to be. In fact, it has been getting worse. Those on whom you have been depending are getting fewer in number because people are growing weary of helping out. This is a wonderful lesson from life that something is wrong in your expectations.

TASK: Go through your lists and ask yourself who you are hoping will help you. The lesson to learn is that it is your job to help yourself to the very best of your ability before you expect others to join in.

SESSION 2

EXERCISE 1B – PERSONAL COMMITMENT, HANGING ON

Session 2 will focus you on the absence of goals in your life. Goals are necessary because they create focus and focus is the first step in positive change. Let's get started.

Consider your goals for your personal life. Where do you want to be in one year? Five years? Ten years? It doesn't matter where you are right now; until you set personal goals, your life will continue to slip toward chaos. When was the last time you had a goal? It may have been for your career, your marriage, your weight, or almost anything. Reflect on how long it has been and write down the results of not having goals.

TASK: Give yourself a grade from A (great at making goals) to F (never make goals). Write down the reasons you gave yourself that grade.

EXERCISE 2B – PERSONAL COMMITMENT, HANGING ON

Now, we want you to consider specifically any goals you have for your work or school life. What goals have you had in the past? How long ago did you have them? Write them down. Were they clear? Where they ambitious? What happened to them? Since goals set the trajectory and pace of change, the absence of clear goals has likely interfered with your ability to build a satisfying and meaningful educational or vocational life for yourself.

TASK: Reflect on the lack of clear goals and the implication.

EXERCISE 3B – PERSONAL COMMITMENT, HANGING ON

Next, we want you to consider goals for the important relationships in your life. What goals have you had for your marriage or partnership? What goals do you have for your friendships? For your social life? Which of your goals were met and which fell by the wayside? When they weren't fulfilled, what happened? Rich relationships are built on clear goals because goals guide our choices.

TASK: Write how your relationships might have been richer if you had set clear goals.

EXERCISE 4B – PERSONAL COMMITMENT, HANGING ON

Finally, we want you to consider goals you may or may not have for your finances. This is one of the places where many people struggle the most. It is easy to want things that you can't afford and to get into trouble by using credit that you can't afford to repay. Financial goals would allow you to live within your means and to expand your income such that you can purchase things that you want.

TASK: List any financial goals you may have had in the past and what happened to them. Do you still have financial goals? Do you find them to be useful?

SESSION 3

EXERCISE 1C – PERSONAL COMMITMENT, HANGING ON

You may have noticed that you either had hardly any goals for your life and/or the ones you had were not very clear or specific. Goals are critical because they set the course for your life. Plans are necessary because they put your goals into action. It is likely that you may not be very good at planning.

TASK: Give yourself a grade from A (I am extremely good at making plans) to F (I am horrible at making plans). After you have given yourself a grade, write down the reasons you have given yourself that grade.

EXERCISE 2C – PERSONAL COMMITMENT, HANGING ON

Creating milestones. Exercise 2 is designed to assist you in making your goals more useful. Goals can be daunting because they often demand substantial change that will require effort over a long period of time. In order to maintain the focus and motivation to stick with your goals, you will need to break them down into smaller goals we call milestones. Milestones are simply shorter-term outcomes that lead toward your goal. For example, if you were going to train for a marathon, your milestones might be running 5 miles, 10 miles, 15 miles, and 20 miles. You could also decide when you need to reach each milestone in order to be prepared to run the marathon.

TASK: Take one of your goals and create some milestones. Work on this over the next week until your milestones seem reasonable and adequate to get you to your goal on time.

EXERCISE 3C – PERSONAL COMMITMENT, HANGING ON

Even milestones can be too complex and long-term to sustain motivation. This week we want you to break your milestones into action steps. Action steps are discrete activities that are necessary to reach your milestone. If you are going to run 5 miles (your first milestone), you may need to: 1. Buy running shoes, 2. Plan when you will run, and 3. Determine your route. Once you have your action steps listed, you should put them on your calendar. This will give you a clear and complete plan to achieve your goal.

TASK: This week you can create your action steps and put them on your calendar.

EXERCISE 4C – PERSONAL COMMITMENT, HANGING ON

Finally, put your action steps on your calendar. This seems like such a simple step but it is one that is too often overlooked. The best plans fall apart if you don't put them into play. In order to move your plan into action, write the day and time when you will complete each one. Start every day by reviewing your calendar. Your action items should be a high priority. Make sure they get done. Mark each one off and look forward to the next one.

TASK: Make it a habit to run your life based on the priorities you have created with your action plan. Now, get out your calendar and get to work.

SESSION 4

EXERCISE 1D – PERSONAL COMMITMENT, HANGING ON

Grade yourself on self-discipline. Even the best plans are of little value if you lack the discipline to follow through on them.

TASK: We want you to do a self-assessment as to your ability to discipline yourself to do that which you have committed to do. Give yourself an A if you are 100 percent reliable. You follow through on every action item on your calendar. Give yourself a B if you follow through on most of them. Give yourself a C if you follow through on only about half of your action items. Give yourself a D if you follow through on some and an F if you never follow through. Anything less than a B is a problem. If you gave yourself a lower grade, consider why you don't follow through. Did you not care about the goal in the first place? Did you care about your goal but forgot to check your calendar? Did you check your calendar but were distracted by something else? Did you start to execute on your action items but became discouraged and gave up? Identifying the issue that undermines your discipline is very important.

EXERCISE 2D – PERSONAL COMMITMENT, HANGING ON

Getting started. The first step in self-discipline is to take a first step. Talk is cheap. Nothing changes until you make a change. It doesn't need to be a big change, but it must be some action that moves in the direction of your goals. Notice any tendency you might have to think about changing without doing anything. Notice how you talk to yourself and note any self-talk that discourages you from getting started. Pick any one of your goals and determine your first step.

TASK: Write down when you will take that first step. Visualize how you will do it, how it will feel, and what will come from having completed it. Now, follow through. Congratulations. You have taken the first step on your journey toward a more meaningful life.

EXERCISE 3D – PERSONAL COMMITMENT, HANGING ON

Sticking with it. Now that you have taken your first step, you need to focus on maintaining your forward momentum. One of the most important skills in continuing your progress is to keep your focus only on the very next step. When your goal requires significant change or will take a long time to achieve, it can be easy to become discouraged and to quit. But if you focus only on the very next step, it is not so hard. Use your practice from last week to visualize your next step and then take it.

TASK: This week we want you to practice appreciating yourself every time you complete one of your action steps. Noting your success and progress is a helpful way to encourage yourself to keep moving forward. Practice this week taking one step, appreciating yourself, and then planning the next one. This should become a regular habit in your life.

EXERCISE 4D – PERSONAL COMMITMENT, HANGING ON

Overcoming obstacles. No one achieves their goals without encountering obstacles from time to time. Usually they are unexpected and may get in the way of your progress. We want you to expect obstacles so when they come you aren't surprised. Next, accept that you may need to modify your plan while you find a way around or over your obstacle. Learn to notice the obstacle, step back to consider how the obstacle will interfere with your goal, and then do some creative problem solving. What options do you have in dealing with the obstacle? What help do you need? How can you alter your plan to work around the obstacle but keep moving forward to your goal?

TASK: Pick one obstacle you have encountered and see what you can do to create a plan to work around it.

FACTOR – PERSONAL COMMITMENT

The capacity to voluntarily choose your goals, to properly manage your behaviors, and to discipline yourself to follow through on your plan.

SELF-ASSESSED RATING - ERODING

You are not sufficiently skilled at setting goals, making realistic plans, or having the discipline to follow through on them.

SESSION 1

EXERCISE 1A – PERSONAL COMMITMENT, ERODING

Your life is eroding at least partly because you are not sufficiently skilled at creating effective goals, making realistic plans, and/or having the discipline to follow through. These exercises are designed to assist you in identifying where you might be deficient and to provide some skill development that will assist you in improving the quality of your life. Let's start by asking you to make an honest assessment. How effective are you at using goals and plans to improve your life?

TASK: Answer the following questions honestly: *In what areas of my life do I have goals? In what areas do I not have goals? Where have goals been effective? Where have they not and why?* Reviewing your history of goal setting and follow through can be very insightful in helping you to understand where you get stuck.

EXERCISE 2A – PERSONAL COMMITMENT, ERODING

Now let's focus your attention on your commitment to goal setting. Unless you see the value of setting goals, it is not likely that you will improve your ability to create and utilize goal setting. Stephen Covey wrote in *The 7 Habits of Highly Effective People* that all things are created twice. First, they are created in your mind. Then, they are created in your life. In other words, you must envision what you want before you will apply the energy to make it happen. He was talking about setting goals.

TASK: Look back through your life and make a list of the things you have created—at the successes you have achieved. Now, go back and see if you can remember when you first formed the vision or set the goal for that achievement. It is likely that almost all of your successes were preceded by setting a goal. This link is important to see so you will be encouraged to be more robust in setting goals.

EXERCISE 3A – PERSONAL COMMITMENT, ERODING

Now, let's focus on the areas of your life that are in disrepair. You are eroding because parts of your life are moving in the wrong direction.

TASK: List those areas where your life is eroding. Next to each, see if you are aware of a goal you have for that area. You might be surprised to discover that you don't have a goal. Or, you may have goal that hasn't seemed to help you. Either is okay. We just want you to become more aware of where you have and haven't set goals and how they have or haven't helped you.

EXERCISE 4A – PERSONAL COMMITMENT, ERODING

Finally, let's start the process of setting goals in the areas of your life that are in disarray. Goals start with dreams.

TASK: Take some time and create a dream for the life you want, especially in the weak areas. Be specific and write down whatever comes to mind. For example, if you aren't making enough money, write down the kind of job that would be exciting for you to have and how much money you would be bringing home. Dreams don't have to be practical but they should be inspiring. Your dreams are the foundation of your goals.

SESSION 2

EXERCISE 1B – PERSONAL COMMITMENT, ERODING

In this session we will focus on the basic skills you need to develop to create effective goals. The first is dreaming. As we pointed out in an earlier exercise, before you create anything new in your life, you must first create it in your mind. It starts with becoming clear with what you want. Take one area in which your life is eroding. It might be your friendships, finances, career, health, or any other area that needs to be stronger. Take some time to dream a dream for that area of your life. What would you like this area of your life to be like? Notice that you might immediately begin to doubt that you can have what you want and begin to pare back your dream. Try to resist it. Let your dreams be dreams. You don't have to see how they will come to be. We are asking you to release your imagination and will.

TASK: Revise your dream every day this week to add new thoughts and details.

EXERCISE 2B – PERSONAL COMMITMENT, ERODING

The second skill in creating powerful goals is to be concrete. Turn your dream into something that is clear and, if possible, measurable. Instead of saying that you want more friends, a better goal is that you want ten new friends in the next six months. Or, instead of saying you want a bigger house, a better goal is a three-bedroom split-level with a garage. Unclear goals are actually more difficult to achieve than are clear ones. Clear goals shape the path to achieve them. If your goal is to have more friends, we don't know if that is one new friend or a hundred new friends. We don't know if you want to have new friends tomorrow or in ten years. If your goal is to have ten new friends in the next six months, we have enough details to begin to formulate a plan.

TASK: Sit down with your dream and make it as clear and concrete as possible. Review it every day for the next week and sharpen up the clarity.

EXERCISE 3B – PERSONAL COMMITMENT, ERODING

The third skill is to make your goal visible to you on a regular basis. You can do this by writing it down, cutting out pictures to represent your goal, or finding some other way to keep it in front of you on a regular basis. If you want to lose 20 lbs. by the summer, you might buy that smaller bathing suit and leave it on the hanger on the back of your bedroom door. Every morning and evening you will see that suit and remember your goal. Or, you could make a collage with pictures of homes like the one you want to buy in the next two years. Put it on your refrigerator door so that every time you go into the kitchen you are reminded of your goal. Keeping your goal visible is a way of beginning to shift your mind and energy toward the path to achieve your dream. The more you imagine yourself having what you want, the more you unleash the energy and discipline necessary to achieve it.

TASK: Turn your goal into something visible and compelling. Put it somewhere you will see it on a regular basis.

EXERCISE 4B – PERSONAL COMMITMENT, ERODING

Finally, share your goal with your friends. There is tremendous power in accountability. When you share your goal with your friends, you are setting an expectation that you will achieve it. They will ask you about your goal and how you are doing accomplishing it. Their encouragement might get you over a period of doubt or discouragement. Ask your friends to check in with you often and to encourage you to keep moving forward until you have been successful.

TASK: Make a list of the people with whom you want to share your goal. This week go to each of them and openly share your goal for your life.

SESSION 3

EXERCISE 1C – PERSONAL COMMITMENT, ERODING

In Session 2 we were introducing you to the concept of creating meaningful goals for aspects of your life. Some of these concepts may be new for you and may take a while for you to master. Now, we are shifting to the next step: turning your goals into useful plans. Even if you are good at creating goals, until you know how to convert them into useful plans, nothing much will change. Let's start by asking you to assess how often you create plans.

TASK: Take time to look back through your life and to consider your accomplishments. List all the major ones. Check every one for which you had constructed a plan. You may have lost 20 lbs. Did you have a plan or did it just seem to happen? Can you see from your past that planning has been a useful tool in creating positive change?

EXERCISE 2C – PERSONAL COMMITMENT, ERODING

Now, we want you to see how useful your plans have been. Perhaps you created plans that just didn't work. You may not know the reason they failed, but your history with planning doesn't encourage you to plan more.

TASK: Make a list of any plans you created in the past that didn't work. Look for patterns that might indicate the reason they failed. Consider this list of potential problems with your plans: 1. They weren't specific, 2. They were too ambitious, 3. You didn't write them down, 4. You hardly ever referred to them, 5. They were unclear, and 6. They weren't adequately thorough.

EXERCISE 3C – PERSONAL COMMITMENT, ERODING

The first step in establishing an effective plan is to create milestones. Milestones indicate where you want to be by when. For example, if your goal was to save $10,000 in five years, your milestones might be you will have saved $2,000 by the end of the first year, $5,000 by the middle of the third year and so on. Milestones are markers that let you know you are on pace to achieve your goal.

TASK: Take one goal for your life and create milestones. Make sure they are measurable and, even if difficult, seem achievable.

EXERCISE 4C – PERSONAL COMMITMENT, ERODING

The next step in making effective plans is to create action steps for each milestone. If my first milestone is to save $2,000 by the end of the year, what will I do to make that happen? Action steps might include opening a savings account at the bank and depositing $40 each week into that account. If you can't save that much, another action step might be asking for a raise or looking for another job. Notice that each action step is a concrete deliverable. It is something you are able to do. It is important to create the series of action steps that, if you fulfill each, should get you to your next milestone. Each action step needs to have a date (and perhaps even a time) when it will be completed. Of course, things can happen that can temporarily derail you. For that reason, your plan needs to be a living document—one that will be periodically revised based on changes.

TASK: Go back to your milestones and create action steps. Review them every day this week and add detail.

SESSION 4

EXERCISE 1D – PERSONAL COMMITMENT, ERODING

Finally, put your action steps on your calendar. This seems like such a simple step but it is one that is too often overlooked. The best plans fall apart if you don't put them into play. In order to move your plan into action, write the day and time when you will complete each one.

TASK: Start every day by reviewing your calendar. Your action items should be a high priority. Make sure they get done. Mark each one off and look forward to the next one. Make it a habit to run your life based on the priorities you have created with your action plan. Now, get out your calendar and get to work.

EXERCISE 2D – PERSONAL COMMITMENT, ERODING

Even the best plans are of little value if you lack the discipline to follow through on them.

TASK: We want you to do a self-assessment as to your ability to discipline yourself to do what you have committed to do. Give yourself an A if you are 100 percent reliable. You follow through on every action item on your calendar. Give yourself a B if you follow through on most of them. Give yourself a C if you follow through on only about half of your action items. Give yourself a D if you follow through on some and an F if you never follow through. Anything less than a B is a problem. If you gave yourself a lower grade, consider why you don't follow through. Did you not care about the goal in the first place? Did you care about your goal but forgot to check your calendar? Did you check your calendar but were distracted by something else? Did you start to execute on your action items but became discouraged and gave up? Identifying the issue that undermines your discipline is very important.

EXERCISE 3D – PERSONAL COMMITMENT, ERODING

If you discovered that you lacked motivation to follow through on your action items, it is highly likely that you created the wrong goals. They might be goals you thought you should have but they weren't goals you truly cared about. This is a critical distinction. It is very difficult to follow through unless you are genuinely motivated. For example, you might think it is a good idea to lose 20 lbs. but you want to eat donuts more than you want to lose weight. If that is the case, don't set a goal of losing 20 lbs. You are only setting yourself up for failure. It is better to enjoy eating donuts until the time losing weight becomes more important.

TASK: Go back to your list of goals. Decide which ones you truly care about. Cross out all of the others. Now, focus only on those that remain on your list.

EXERCISE 4D – PERSONAL COMMITMENT, ERODING

Goal setting and follow through need to be practiced. The more you practice, the better you will get. It is often wise to start with small, easy-to-achieve goals.

TASK: Create milestones and action items for those. Follow through until you have achieved your goal. Get used to how it feels to set goals and achieve them. Then, take on more challenging goals. Usually, those that require a longer time to achieve or that require more change in our lives are the more difficult ones. Gradually take on more difficult ones as you gain greater confidence in your ability to use goal-setting to shape your life.

FACTOR – PERSONAL COMMITMENT

The capacity to voluntarily choose your goals, to properly manage your behaviors, and to discipline yourself to follow through on your plan.

SELF-ASSESSED RATING - TREADING WATER

There are some areas of your life where you have been effective at setting goals and following through, but there are other areas where you have not been as effective.

SESSION 1

EXERCISE 1A – PERSONAL COMMITMENT, TREADING WATER

You are treading water at least partly because you are not sufficiently skilled at creating effective goals, making realistic plans, and/or having the discipline to follow through. These exercises are designed to assist you in identifying where you might be deficient and to provide some skill development that will assist you in improving the quality of your life.

TASK: Let's start by asking you to make an honest assessment. In what areas of your life have you been effective at setting goals and following through? In what areas have you not been very effective at setting goals and following through? Now that you have these two lists, look at the one where you haven't been effective. What is going on here? Can you identify a pattern or common theme? You might be effective in setting goals for your finances but not for your physical fitness. What is it about your physical fitness that hangs you up? Insights such as these are critical for getting yourself unstuck. If you can't see a pattern, consider a few sessions with one of our coaches.

EXERCISE 2A – PERSONAL COMMITMENT, TREADING WATER

One of the common issues that undermine the effective use of goals to shape your life is having goals that you really don't care about. They might be goals you think you should have but they aren't goals you truly care about. This is a critical distinction. It is very difficult to follow through unless you are genuinely motivated. For example, you might think it is a good idea to lose 20 lbs. but you want to eat donuts more than you want to lose weight. If that is the case, don't set a goal of losing 20 lbs. You are only setting yourself up for failure. It is better to enjoy eating donuts until the time losing weight becomes more important.

TASK: Go back to your list of goals. Decide which ones you truly care about. Cross out all of the others. Now, focus only on those that remain on your list.

EXERCISE 3A – PERSONAL COMMITMENT, TREADING WATER

A second place where your goals may have gone astray is that you have failed to create new goals for your life. Many of us dream about our lives when we are children, and it is those dreams that shape the accomplishments of our lives. But when we achieve many of those goals, it is easy to become complacent and to stop dreaming dreams and setting goals for the future. We call this the "danger zone." Life is not bad enough to force you to set new goals. Nor do you have any dreams that require significant change. The danger is that even though life around you is changing, your life is not. Eventually, the lack of forward movement will lead to backward drift. Your life will begin to erode.

TASK: Take 15 minutes every day this week and dream some dreams about your future. What do you want that you don't have? What do you want to give up that is holding you back? Make a list.

EXERCISE 4A – PERSONAL COMMITMENT, TREADING WATER

Take out your list of goals from last week. We want you to identify the one that would be most beneficial in getting you unstuck and moving forward in your life. Once you have picked it, create a very clear outcome for that area of your life. If it is financial, pick the amount of money you want to be making and by what date. If it is relational, write down that you will have found your life partner and the date when that will be achieved. It might seem strange to pick such a clear and concrete goal for an area of your life that has been stuck, but goals such as these have tremendous power to create change.

TASK: Now, review your goal every day until it feels possible.

SESSION 2

EXERCISE 1B – PERSONAL COMMITMENT, TREADING WATER

Finally, share your goal with at least five people who care about you.

TASK: List the people you can count on to be supportive and to believe that you can make positive changes in this area where you have been stuck. Plan time to meet with each of them to share your goal. Ask them to support you by asking about your progress and encouraging you to achieve it. Engaging your support network is a powerful tool to help you get unstuck and moving forward.

EXERCISE 2B – PERSONAL COMMITMENT, TREADING WATER

Now that you have a goal that will improve your life and about which you are excited, it is time to turn it into a plan. Plans are like the blueprints for a house. You might have a great picture of the house you want to build, but you need step-by-step plans to actually build it. There is always a very first thing that needs to be done followed by the next thing. It is only when you create and follow that order that the house gets built.

TASK: Take out your goal. It is clear what you want to create. Now, decide how long you want to take to create it. This may vary depending on the goal. It will take a lot longer to lose 50 lbs. than it will to lose 10. Setting the right timeframe is very important. If it is too short, you set yourself up for discouragement. If it is too long, you may lose interest. It is okay to push yourself a bit here but don't be too unrealistic. Write down a specific date for when you want to have achieved your goal.

EXERCISE 3B – PERSONAL COMMITMENT, TREADING WATER

Now that you have an end date to achieve your goal, you need to create some milestones with due dates. Going back to the house illustration, if you want it finished in three months, you can more easily decide exactly what needs to be done and when. For example, surveying the lot is the first step. Then, you need to excavate. Third is pouring the foundation and so on. For the house to be finished in three months, the surveying needs to be done by the day after tomorrow, the excavation by the end of next week, and so on. List every milestone in the fulfillment of your goal. Be very clear. If it is losing 20 lbs., you may first need to investigate a diet program, then sign up for one, and then plan your meals, etc.

TASK: Once you have your entire list of milestones, place dates next to each. Make sure your milestones are a reasonable plan to reach your goal.

EXERCISE 4B – PERSONAL COMMITMENT, TREADING WATER

Next, break down your milestones into action items. This might seem unnecessary but it is extremely helpful. It might be one thing to decide that the foundation needs to be finished by next week. But, there are many things that need to happen in order to complete the foundation. Block must be ordered. Subcontractors need to be hired. Cement must be scheduled. These and many other issues need to be organized to reach the milestone. If any is missed, the whole project is at risk. So, take each of your milestones and list every action step necessary to complete them. For example, if your first milestone is finding a diet program, your first action item is to do an online search. Next, you make a list of programs. Then, you visit your top three. Finally, you are ready to pick one.

TASK: Take each of your milestones and break them down into action items. Take all week to make this complete. Place a day (and/or time) when each will be completed.

SESSION 3

EXERCISE 1C – PERSONAL COMMITMENT, TREADING WATER

Calendaring. One of the easiest steps to underestimate in using goal setting to create a positive future is simply keeping your action items in front of you every day. Life is busy for everyone. There is always more than enough to do. You need a plan to make sure you stay focused on your goal each day and week until it is fulfilled. The best way we have found to do this is to put each action item on your calendar. You have created a blueprint for change that has target dates. Now, write those action items into specific time slots on your calendar. These should become top-priority items. Start every day by reviewing your calendar. Shift items as necessary but make sure your action items have sufficient time allocated in order to complete them.

TASK: At the end of each day, review your calendar and check that you have completed your action items. Make this a habit. It will help to keep you on track.

EXERCISE 2C – PERSONAL COMMITMENT, TREADING WATER

Being methodical. Self-discipline is a critical skill to cultivate if you are going to master goal setting for creating a powerful life. The words are clear; it is about disciplining yourself. It is important to think about this as a skill you practice and refine such that you become better and better at self-discipline.

TASK: Evaluate your life right now. Write down those areas where you exercise good self-discipline and those where you don't. Notice that your life is stronger in those areas where you apply self-discipline. Ask yourself why you haven't been disciplined in the other areas and if you are ready to apply self-discipline now.

EXERCISE 3C – PERSONAL COMMITMENT, TREADING WATER

Saying yes to what you want. One of the ways to increase your self-discipline is to stay laser-focused on what you want and why you want it. The more clearly you see the benefits of your goal, the more motivated you will be to do whatever it takes to keep moving forward. There are several ways you keep focused on the benefits of what you want. First, take 15 minutes each day to meditate on how much better things will be when you have achieved your goal. Visualize yourself having lost those 20 lbs. or driving the car you are saving to get. Let yourself feel the satisfaction and joy that comes from the achievement.

TASK: Practice this every day.

EXERCISE 4C – PERSONAL COMMITMENT, TREADING WATER

Saying no to distractions. A second way you improve your self-discipline is to say no to distractions. Sometimes it is difficult to persevere toward a goal. Distractions pop up that will tempt you away from your commitment. For example, you are working toward your plan to get a promotion by putting in extra hours to work on special projects. Your friends have tickets to the ballgame and want you to go. It would be so easy to take the evening off. Here is the time to practice saying no to distractions. Focus on this moment. You have a decision to make. One has short-term gains at long-term cost (the ballgame). The other has short-term cost (not going to the game) but long-term gain (the promotion). Make the right decision for this moment.

TASK: Practice making these decisions and they will become easier to see and to make.

SESSION 4

EXERCISE 1D – PERSONAL COMMITMENT, TREADING WATER

Harnessing positive momentum. Encourage your new ability to move your life forward by celebrating small wins. Every action step is an opportunity for you to survey your progress and to congratulate yourself for harnessing your self-discipline to improve your life. A celebration as simple as your self-congratulation will be a big motivator to keep moving forward. Achieving milestones is another opportunity to celebrate, perhaps in a bigger way. Reward yourself by going to a movie that you wanted to see or having a special meal when you achieve a milestone.

TASK: Practice noticing your achievement, celebrating, resting, and renewing your commitment to take on the next milestone. That pattern allows you to keep moving forward without wearing out.

EXERCISE 2D – PERSONAL COMMITMENT, TREADING WATER

Create a community of growing people. Begin building a network of people who are using goal setting to improve their lives. Competing with each other in hitting milestones can be a way of adding motivation to your plan of action. Not only can you encourage each other, but your network can review each other's milestones and action plans and add insights and details. The better the plan, the easier it is to keep. The more encouragement and assistance you have, the more successful you will be in fulfilling your goals.

TASK: List the names of people you can add to your network. Be on the lookout each day for people you can add.

EXERCISE 3D – PERSONAL COMMITMENT, TREADING WATER

Build on your success. You have been treading water because you haven't taken on whatever was necessary to move your life forward. Now that you are working this plan, you should notice some positive changes. Your life will begin having forward momentum. Momentum is important because it is much easier to direct your life when it is changing than when it is standing still. The changes you are making get you used to the process of change, which should become a natural and regular part of your life.

TASK: Step back and assess the results of the work you have been doing. Are you proud of yourself? Doesn't that feel good? Do you see that you can make positive changes in your life by planning? Learning to appreciate yourself and harness kind and supportive energy is critical to sustain continued growth.

EXERCISE 4D – PERSONAL COMMITMENT, TREADING WATER

Creating your future. Don't stop creating goals when you have achieved your current ones. Remember that your life is dynamic. If you aren't moving forward, it is likely that you are sliding backward. There is never a time to be finished with dreaming, goal setting, creating milestones and action items, and disciplining yourself to execute on your plans.

TASK: Create a wish list of goals that are ahead of you. You don't have to turn them into plans today, but they are ideas you return to every quarter to assess if it is time to put them into action. Keep moving forward.

FACTOR – PERSONAL COMMITMENT

The capacity to voluntarily choose your goals, to properly manage your behaviors, and to discipline yourself to follow through on your plan.

SELF-ASSESSED RATING - GROWING

You have mastered the ability to effectively set goals and follow through on achieving them in all areas of your life but one, which is keeping you from thriving.

SESSION 1

EXERCISE 1A – PERSONAL COMMITMENT, GROWING

Your life is growing because, for the most part, you have mastered the ability to effectively form meaningful goals and to execute them consistently. However, you aren't thriving because there is some area of your life where your goal setting and execution is getting derailed. The purpose of these exercises is to assist you in identifying that area, better understanding why you have not yet mastered it, and how you can break free. Let's start by asking you to write down where you want to be successful but aren't.

TASK: List any issues that come to mind both big and small. This should be a short list and may very well consist of just one item. If it is longer, see if you can reduce your list to one theme. We want you to focus on the one thing that will move you toward fully thriving.

EXERCISE 2A – PERSONAL COMMITMENT, GROWING

Now, let's go back to the one thing you wrote down and review your history with that area of your life. Were you successful in this area in the past but are not now? If so, what happened? If not, what has gotten in the way of your success?

TASK: Pay attention to any patterns that have inhibited your ability to effectively move forward in this area. Perhaps you have created a very successful life with the exception of your intimate relationships that always end suddenly and dramatically. Maybe you grew up in a family where your parents didn't get along and didn't learn how to form close and stable relationships. Usually, there is some historic issue that undermines successful goal setting when you are unable to move forward in only one area of your life. If you need assistance in identifying your issue, please call on one of your trusted friends for assistance.

EXERCISE 3A – PERSONAL COMMITMENT, GROWING

Take another look at this one area where you have failed to successfully make and execute your goal. List any obstacles that stand in your way. Perhaps you are afraid of the consequences of moving forward in this area of your life. For example, getting a new job might require relocating and you are concerned that this would be too stressful for your family. You have been settling for less than you want because you haven't known how or have been unwilling to address that obstacle.

TASK: Take 15 minutes each day to review this exercise and see if other obstacles or issues come to mind.

EXERCISE 4A – PERSONAL COMMITMENT, GROWING

One of the most important tools you have to break old patterns and to overcome obstacles is your imagination. If you can imagine what you want, you can create it. Imagination is powerful because it opens up new possibilities that may not be easy to see when you are hemmed in by some old point of view or some obstacle that seems insurmountable.

TASK: Go back to the issue that you want to resolve and imagine that you have achieved whatever you want in this area of your life. Don't be practical or reasonable. Be big in your imagination. Write it down and read it three times each day for the next week.

SESSION 2

EXERCISE 1B – PERSONAL COMMITMENT, GROWING

Either/or thinking. One of the traps that can limit your ability to set effective goals in this one area is "either/or" thinking. It works like this, "If I get that new job and need to move, my spouse will be mad at me forever. I can either have that new job or a happy spouse." Because you believe you must choose between two options, you get stuck. A new way and better way of thinking is "both/and." Rather than imagining you must choose between two things, create a goal that includes good outcomes for both options. "I will get the new job and my spouse will be delighted." This is a goal that can get you unstuck.

TASK: Go back to the place where you have been ineffective in moving forward. Check to see if you have any "either/or" thinking that has been getting in your way. If so, create a goal that gets you everything you want.

EXERCISE 2B – PERSONAL COMMITMENT, GROWING

In order for your goal setting to be put into use, you must turn it into a meaningful action plan. Goals can actually become discouraging if you don't create a clear path for how they can be achieved. If you aren't a runner and set a goal to run a marathon, it might seem impossible to prepare. But, if you use a training plan that outlines exactly how far you will run every day until the race, the goal becomes more reasonable to achieve. Now that you have clarity about the breakthrough you want to create in your life so that you are thriving, turn it into a plan. The first step is to create reasonable milestones. Milestones are like road markers. They map your progress. A marathon is a little over 26 miles. Training milestones might be a 5-, 10-, 15-, and 20-mile run. You know you can't run even 1 mile today, but when you hit each milestone, you will pause, look back at how far you have come, celebrate your success, and recommit to the next phase of your training. Milestones allow you to break a big goal down into meaningful sub goals upon which it is easier to stay focused and motivated to achieve.

TASK: Go back to your goal and create milestones.

EXERCISE 3B – PERSONAL COMMITMENT, GROWING

The second part of effective milestones is establishing dates for when you will hit them. Setting due dates allows you to create a pace that is realistic. It should not be so slow that you lose interest because you don't see enough progress. It should not be so aggressive that you can't keep up. You should think carefully about all that you have going on in your life and how much energy and effort it will take to accomplish your goal. Then, set dates for your milestones. For example, if you want to run that marathon six months from now, you know you have six months of training to prepare your body to run 26 miles. Hence you probably want to make sure you hit your last milestone (running 26 miles) about one week before the race. You may set your 15-mile milestone two months before the race. Your 10-mile milestone might be set four months before the race, and your 5-mile milestone five months before the race. Now you can see how fast you will need to progress in order to be ready to run the marathon.

TASK: Go back to your milestones and set appropriate dates for each one.

EXERCISE 4B – PERSONAL COMMITMENT, GROWING

Even milestones can be too big to be optimal. If you aren't a runner and want to be able to run 5 miles in one month, how will you get there? There are likely to be more things than you imagine to even reach that goal. This is the role for action steps. Action steps are very discrete but critical actions that must be taken to reach your milestones. For example, if you are going to train for the marathon even before your first jog around the block, you need to find a training plan. Your first action step might be going online and downloading one that seems to fit you the best. The next step might be going to the store and buying a new pair of running shoes. The third step might be planning when you will schedule your runs. The first three steps didn't include any running. A good plan includes all of the action steps necessary to reach each milestone. Again, a date (and/or time) should be established for each one.

TASK: Go back to your milestones and create action steps for each one. Feel free to modify your action steps as you learn more information.

SESSION 3

EXERCISE 1C – PERSONAL COMMITMENT, GROWING

The next step is to get your action steps into your schedule. You have mapped out all of the steps you need to take to reach your goal and when you want to be at each milestone. But it is likely that you have a busy life with plenty of things to take up your time. How you allocate your time is critical to being successful in breaking through toward thriving. Your action steps should be put on your calendar so that you know when you will accomplish each one. It can be a significant shift to plan your day based on what is most important to accomplish rather than what is most immediate.

TASK: We challenge you to organize your schedule based on the five most important things that need to get done each day. Start each week placing those things on your calendar and giving each one sufficient time to be accomplished. Plan each item at the time when it is most conducive for you to address it. Start each day by reviewing your calendar, making whatever adjustments are necessary, and then using the priority on your calendar to determine how you use your time. Take out your calendar and get to work.

EXERCISE 2C – PERSONAL COMMITMENT, GROWING

Now you have all of the tools in place to break through that one area that has been holding you back. You have a clear goal that you are motivated to achieve. You have faced any old patterns and obstacles that have been getting in your way. You have created a clear and compelling plan with milestones and action steps. And every action step and milestone is on your calendar. None of these things will help at all unless you discipline yourself to follow through. One of the best ways to build self-discipline is to stay focused on only the next step of your plan. You don't have to discipline yourself to six months of training for the marathon. You need to discipline yourself only to complete today's run. A long journey is completed one step at a time. As you learn to focus only on the next step, you will find that completing each step makes it easier to take on the next one. Completing today's step strengthens your resolve to tackle tomorrow's.

TASK: Every day this week, practice focusing only on that day's action item and making sure you complete it. Don't give yourself any slack or make up any excuses why you can't. Get used to completing every one.

EXERCISE 3C – PERSONAL COMMITMENT, GROWING

Using support. Another helpful tool in strengthening your self-discipline is to form a small group of friends who hold each other accountable for executing their action items. Peer support is one of the most powerful ways to get past those times when you lose focus or waver on your commitment to yourself. Check in with your friends every day and share the action step you have accomplished. Ask for support when you know you will be going through an especially stressful or difficult period. Periodically meet face-to-face to share updates on your goals and plans. You will find this group of close friends to be one of the great sources of strength in your life.

TASK: Take this week to list the people you will invite to your group. Make the invitations in person where possible. Schedule times when you will talk and meet in person.

EXERCISE 4C – PERSONAL COMMITMENT, GROWING

Celebration. A final tool to assist you in your self-discipline is celebration. Celebration is taking the time to review the progress you have made, reward yourself in some way, rest, and recommit to the next step of your plan. Celebration helps you break your goal into a series of journeys rather than one very long one. One good place to celebrate is at each milestone. Think of something you can do for yourself that feels like a special reward. It could be something like a nice dinner.

TASK: Review all of the action steps you have taken and the accomplishments you have achieved to that point. Let yourself feel satisfied with your success. You may even take a day off from your program (just make sure you schedule this on your calendar). Then, look at the next milestone and series of action steps and commit to completing them. This pattern of committing, achieving, celebrating, resting, and recommitting will keep you on track.

SESSION 4

EXERCISE 1D – PERSONAL COMMITMENT, GROWING

Drift. No one has flawless self-discipline. Things come up, you lose motivation or become distracted, and your plan falls by the wayside. We call that drifting. This week we want you to notice where you are drifting. Review all areas of your life and make a list of any places where you have drifted off of your goals. Be as complete as possible. When you are finished, we want you to read your list and to love yourself. One of the bad habits that is easy to fall into is to be harsh with yourself when you drift. It is natural to drift. Learning to catch yourself and to be kind and gentle to yourself is the best way to get back on track.

TASK: Practice this week being forgiving of yourself when you drift.

EXERCISE 2D – PERSONAL COMMITMENT, GROWING

Shift. The second skill to master when you catch yourself drifting is to shift. Shifting is about gently calling yourself back to the plan you have established. Life is about constantly drifting and shifting in big and small ways. You might have eaten a donut today even though you have committed to a diet. Don't get discouraged. Just shift back to your diet. Don't worry about yesterday. Don't shame yourself about the donut. Start where you left off and get yourself back on track.

TASK: Use this week to shift back to any plans you have been neglecting.

EXERCISE 3D – PERSONAL COMMITMENT, GROWING

Enjoy the sense of accomplishment and freedom. You have engaged in these exercises to master those few areas that have been keeping you from fully thriving. For the past few weeks, you have been working your plan. Remember that the whole reason for your effort is to make positive changes in your life. It is time for you to notice the impact of your work. Do you see yourself becoming more powerful, clearer, or freer in the area of your life where you were weak or stuck? Thriving is about being the best version of you that you can possibly be. It is so important for you to notice how well you are caring for your life and the results of your labor. Notice the vitality, sense of purpose, and joy you are experiencing. Notice the more powerful and positive impact you are having on others.

TASK: Practice noticing every day this week.

EXERCISE 4D – PERSONAL COMMITMENT, GROWING

Share what you have learned with others. The life skills you have mastered are powerful. It would be good for you to share them with others. Think of the people around you who would benefit from learning how to set and achieve goals. They might be family members, friends, or coworkers. Make a list of the people you think would be receptive. Consider how you might share with them some of the lessons you have learned. One of the best ways is to tell them about the goal you took on and how you achieved it.

TASK: Use your experience as a teaching tool to share all of the lessons you have learned.

EXERCISE SERIES: RELIANCE

FACTOR – RELIANCE

The ability to gain, utilize, and maintain the support of others.

SELF-ASSESSED RATING - HANGING ON

People think of you as unreliable.

SESSION 1

EXERCISE 1A – RELIANCE, HANGING ON

There is no one left. One of the major reasons you are hanging on by your fingernails is that you have failed to gain, utilize, and/or maintain the support of others. Life is a team sport. A vibrant and rich support network can open many doors and provide critical assistance. In Session 1 we are asking you to assess exactly where your skill of reliance has been lacking. The more clearly you see the problem, the more easily you can address it. Let's get started. Make a list of your support network. Write down the name of everyone on whom you can depend for help and support. This may be a very short list. That is okay.

TASK: Review your list every day and add any names that come to mind. You may not be fully aware of the people in your life who want to support you. Expanding your awareness of the good intentions of others is very important.

EXERCISE 2A – RELIANCE, HANGING ON

No one wants to help. Exercise 2 is about understanding why people may and may not want to support you. In order to complete this exercise successfully, you will need the capacity to see yourself accurately and to be completely honest with yourself. If you feel you lack one or both of these skills, please call one of our coaches for assistance. We want you to ask yourself why people might not want to support you.

TASK: Make a list of everything that comes to mind. Now, make a list of all of the reasons people might want to support you. Review both lists from the point of view of the people in your life. How are you getting in your own way? What are you doing or not doing to limit the natural desire of others to want to support you? The following sessions will address some of these issues.

EXERCISE 3A – RELIANCE, HANGING ON

You have wasted the help you were given. Exercise 3 focuses your attention on times when you have wasted the assistance and support others have provided you.

TASK: Make a list of all of the assistance and support you have received in the past. Next to each one, write down the reason you were being given support. What outcome were your supporters trying to create? Then, write down what actually occurred. How often did you fail to achieve the expected outcome? What happened? It is impossible to maintain the support of others if you don't demonstrate the ability to turn their support into real change. How might you be sabotaging your ability to use the assistance you have been given?

EXERCISE 4A – RELIANCE, HANGING ON

You have built few, if any, useful alliances. Exercise 4 invites you to focus on your attitude toward others. Until you completed this assessment, you may not have considered the value of the support others can offer you. You may not have given much, or any, thought to the nature of your support network and how you could build or strengthen it. You may not have thought about the alliances you could build and how they could be mutually beneficial. Consider your attitude about the people in your life.

TASK: Answer the following questions honestly: *How have I acted as if I didn't need or want the support of others? Whom have I known who had the resources to support me but whom I never asked for help? How have I discouraged those who have wanted to support me? How did I think it served me to not have a useful support network?*

SESSION 2

EXERCISE 1B – RELIANCE, HANGING ON

Do what you can for yourself. Session 2 focuses on the fundamentals of building a basic support network. Exercise 1 invites you to do all that you can for yourself. It is difficult for people to want to support you in those things you can do for yourself. If you want help in finding a new job, the people who care about you will want to know that you have taken as many steps as possible before you ask for their assistance. Did you update your résumé? Are you actively applying for jobs that are appropriate and for which you are qualified? Asking people for assistance for things you aren't doing for yourself leads to resentment on their part and the unwillingness to continue to support you.

TASK: Make a list of all of the areas in your life where you are hoping someone else will solve a problem that you aren't actively trying to solve for yourself.

EXERCISE 2B – RELIANCE, HANGING ON

Reach out for help as little as you can. Exercise 2 addresses the second issue in building a support network. Reach out for help as little as you can. This concept piggybacks on Exercise 1. If you ask for too many favors or too much support, people will grow weary of your requests. It is much better to save your requests for assistance for those very key issues that you can't solve yourself. For example, you may have been applying for jobs but your résumé is consistently ignored. Your uncle knows an executive at the company and could ask that executive to help in getting your résumé reviewed. This is an appropriate time to ask for assistance.

TASK: Make a list of as many times when you have requested assistance as you can remember. Take your time and add to this list over the next few days. Now, cross out the ones where you can see you asked too often or for too much. Learn to stop yourself when you are considering asking for help and to wait until it is critically needed.

EXERCISE 3B – RELIANCE, HANGING ON

Be specific. The third basic skill in developing reliance on others is to be specific in your requests. Rather than asking others to solve a general problem, focus your requests on a specific issue. Going back to last week's example, it is far more productive to ask your uncle to talk to his executive friend about getting someone in his company to look at your résumé than to ask your uncle to get you a new job. People generally want to be helpful but they feel best about helping when you are asking for some assistance that is under their control and that they can feel good about accomplishing. Your uncle can talk to his friend. That doesn't guarantee that his friend will honor his request or that you will end up with a job. But it is very important that you build a network of people who enjoy supporting you, and requests that are specific and clear create more goodwill than ones that are vague or general.

TASK: Make a list of areas where you would benefit from having support. For each area, list some clear and specific requests you could make of people in your support network.

EXERCISE 4B – RELIANCE, HANGING ON

Show appreciation. The fourth basic skill in building reliance is showing appreciation. The people who support you want to know that you value them for their interest in you. Whenever they extend themselves to come to your assistance, you have a great opportunity to thank them and to openly express your appreciation for the concern and care. Often people are reluctant to be open with their appreciation or completely take the assistance of others for granted. Practice noticing and expressing appreciation this week.

TASK: Look for at least three opportunities each day when someone does something kind for you and express open appreciation. Notice the effect.

SESSION 3

EXERCISE 1C – RELIANCE, HANGING ON

Be a person people want to be around. Increasing your healthy reliance on others requires the ability to attract and maintain relationships with people who have the ability to assist you. Session 3 invites you to focus on four skills. First, be a person people want to be around. In other words, be an attractive person. Attraction doesn't require physical beauty (although it helps). You can also be beautiful in your attitudes and in your actions. People who are cheerful are delightful to be around. People who are open-minded, generous, and open to share what they have with others more easily attract people into their network of support. It is time for you to assess yourself.

TASK: Make a list of the characteristics you possess that invite people into your support network and which attributes you possess that drive people away. One way to make sure you are being honest with yourself is to ask five people who know you well and will be honest with you to answer those two questions.

EXERCISE 2C – RELIANCE, HANGING ON

Be selective in your associations. The second skill in building even a rudimentary support network is to be selective in who you invite. People can either drag you down or lift you up. They can use what they have to help you move forward or to get in your way. They can delight in your progress or be envious and jealous. It is very important that you invite into your support network only those who have a positive attitude toward you, wish for your success, and have resources they can use to support your life.

TASK: List everyone who is currently in your support network. Next to each name write a + if they are a positive contributor or a - if they tend to be a discouragement or a distraction. Begin detaching from all of the people you rated as a - and begin drawing closer to those with a +.

EXERCISE 3C – RELIANCE, HANGING ON

Focus more on giving to others than getting from them. The third skill in building and maintaining a support network is to focus more on giving to those in your network than taking from them. It is often true in life that whatever you want you should give. If you want support, give it to others. If you want generosity, be generous. That which you give tends to come back to you many times over. In order to be a better giver, it is critical that you make an assessment of all that you have to give. You may underestimate the value of your friendship, encouragement, expertise, talents, and resources.

TASK: List everything you have that could be used to support others. See if you can identify any specific opportunities to better support those to whom you are connected.

EXERCISE 4C – RELIANCE, HANGING ON

Be a person with resources to share. The final skill in building and maintaining a support network is to focus on always gaining more resources for the purpose of sharing them with others. It is easy to get focused on your needs and what is lacking in your life. A far more constructive focus is to keep enriching yourself in ways that allow you to contribute to the lives of others. You might learn a skill because you know someone you could assist if you had that skill. You may make more money because you want to give it to those in need. Enrich yourself for the sole purpose of having more to give away.

TASK: Make a list of all of the things you can do to increase your resources for the betterment of others. Now, put one of those plans into action.

SESSION 4

EXERCISE 1D – RELIANCE, HANGING ON

Use well the help you are given. Session 4 focuses on ways you can sustain and expand your network of people on whom you can rely. Exercise 1 asks you to concentrate on using well the assistance you are given. People who extend their support and assistance want to see that you have benefitted from their assistance. If they think you squandered their help or that it had no positive impact in your life, they will be reluctant to offer you help in the future. Take time now to assess how you have or have not effectively used the assistance you have been given.

TASK: List at least 10 instances where the people who know you tried to help you. Next to each, write the outcome you imagine they wanted to result from their assistance. Now, list what actually occurred. If you didn't benefit from their assistance, what happened? What could you have done differently? Insights you gain from this exercise are important. You will need to make changes in these areas in the future.

EXERCISE 2D – RELIANCE, HANGING ON

Show progress toward getting stronger. Not only do the people who care about you want to see that you put their assistance to use, they also want to see your life getting stronger. You may have borrowed money from your network to buy a car but you don't take care of the car and now it is falling apart. The whole point of their assistance was to see you making progress in taking better care of your life and in being a more productive person. It is your responsibility to use help to make your life as good as it can be.

TASK: List three ways you can take better care of your life that would be meaningful to your support network. Use the skills you have gained from the last few weeks to set goals, milestones, and action steps.

EXERCISE 3D – RELIANCE, HANGING ON

Repay the help you received. The third skill in maintaining your reliance on others is to repay the help you have received. Rather than taking assistance as a gift, it is better to consider it as a loan. You become stronger as you reduce your dependence on others and shift to being a person who rarely needs assistance. You encourage those who helped you when you do all that you can to repay them for their care.

TASK: Make a list of the people who have provided assistance to you. How can you repay them? Sometimes your repayment will be in a different form from the help you received. If you don't know how you can repay them, ask them.

EXERCISE 4D – RELIANCE, HANGING ON

Help others in greater need. The final skill in maintaining healthy reliance on others is to provide support and care to those who are in greater need than you are. Generosity tends to expand the generosity of others toward you. Providing care for those in need also helps you to see your abundance more clearly and to see your needs in a different perspective.

TASK: Make a list of those you know who have needs and make plans to help them.

FACTOR – RELIANCE

The ability to gain, utilize, and maintain the support of others.

SELF-ASSESSED RATING - ERODING

Your network of people on whom you can rely is small and has limited resources.

SESSION 1

EXERCISE 1A – RELIANCE, ERODING

You are using up the people who care for you. You can see that your life is on a downward slide at least partially due to your inability to effectively rely on others. Either your support system isn't adequate or you may have watched it dwindle over time due to issues you don't see or understand. Session 1 is focused on helping you assess the reason for the decline so you are better prepared to address it. Exercise 1 invites you to simply notice what has happened to the people in your life who have tried to assist you.

TASK: Start by making a list of those people and how they tried to help you. Perhaps they offered advice when they thought you were headed off course or loaned you money when you were in a tight spot. The more instances you can list, the more easily you may be able to identify patterns that have limited your effectiveness. Now, look at your list. What happened to those people? Are they still engaged in your life or have they fallen away? If you notice that a large percentage of them have stopped trying to assist you, you can assume that you are doing something that discourages them from continuing to want to assist you. Over the next several weeks, we want you to learn the skills that will help you reverse that pattern.

EXERCISE 2A – RELIANCE, ERODING

You have not used well the assistance you have been given. One of the primary reasons people who care for you become discouraged and stop trying to help may be their judgment that you don't benefit from the assistance they provide. If you take their assistance but fail to put it to good use, they will be less inclined to want to offer help in the future.

TASK: Go back to your list of the people who have tried to help. How many of those events actually produced the desired result and how many fell short? Mark each one accordingly. Look at the list of events that didn't work out as expected. What could you have done to make more of these successful? Looking forward, accept responsibility that every time someone offers to help you they are making an investment in your life and expect a return on that investment. It is your responsibility to make this happen as often as possible.

EXERCISE 3A – RELIANCE, ERODING

You have persisted in habits that cause eroding. A second reason why people become disheartened in their efforts to assist you may be that you persist in habits that undermine your life. Your friends and family want your life to grow progressively stronger and more productive. If you are maintaining any habits that undermine that growth, people will realize that the potential benefit of their assistance is negated by your persistence in unhealthy and unproductive habits. Some of these are clear. Addiction to substances clearly limits your ability to have a productive life. But, being unaware of yourself, not taking responsibility for your life, a commitment to live in drama, persistent gossip and negativity, and many other bad habits are similarly undermining.

TASK: Make a list of all of the habits that need to change in order for you to benefit from the assistance others want to give you.

EXERCISE 4A – RELIANCE, ERODING

You have been too focused on yourself. A third reason people often stop giving assistance may be an excessive focus on yourself and your needs such that you fail to see or appreciate the needs and interests of others. If you are too focused on yourself, you come across to others as if the whole world is about you. All that matters to you are your problems, needs, wants, and frustrations. Excessive self-focus comes across to others as a huge black hole that sucks into it whatever resources come your way and from which nothing good comes back. While people may care about you, they will tire of trying to help you over and over again. You will have exhausted their goodwill toward you and they will go away.

TASK: Make a list of the ways you have been too focused on yourself and your needs and consider how you can expand your concern to include friends, family, and coworkers.

SESSION 2

EXERCISE 1B – RELIANCE, ERODING

Give up blaming others. Session 2 shifts your focus to some of the rudimentary skills necessary to building and maintaining effective reliance on others. You may have some of these skills and others may have fallen into disrepair. Exercise 1 invites you to give up blaming others for all of your problems and shortcomings. Blaming is a common way to avoid taking responsibility for oneself. It might seem counterintuitive but relying on yourself is the most fundamental skill in effectively relying on others. When you are blaming, you are playing the role of the victim and are enticing others to care for you because they don't think you can take care of yourself. While this may lead to short-term care from others, eventually people will tire of taking care of you and will gradually withdraw.

TASK: Keep a list this week of every time you blame someone or something for your circumstances and problems. Now, focus on stopping this habit.

EXERCISE 2B – RELIANCE, ERODING

Give up complaining. A second problematic behavior is complaining. Complaining is akin to blaming except it doesn't hold anyone or anything accountable for your situation. Complaining can become a habit. It can become so chronic that it almost seems as if complaining is actually accomplishing something. In truth, complaining simply vents negative energy. At the end of the day, nothing is better for your complaints.

TASK: Spend this week noticing how often you complain. Complaining is annoying to others. As long as you complain, you will either chase away good-hearted people who genuinely want to help you and/or you will attract others who like to complain. This second group has little to offer you other than sympathy. It is critical that you stop all complaining. Practice.

EXERCISE 3B – RELIANCE, ERODING

Take ownership of your life and doing whatever you can for yourself. Exercise 3 asks you to shift from problematic behaviors to a positive one. Instead of blaming and complaining, take 100 percent ownership for your life. This is your life. If it is good, it is because you took good care of it. If it is bad, it is because you have neglected it. No one owes you anything. If there is something you don't like, it is up to you to fix it. This is a very empowering lesson. You can't afford to hope things will change or to wait for someone to fix your problems.

TASK: Make a list of all of the issues for which you haven't taken full ownership. Now, read each item and practice taking ownership. What will you do to solve each issue? What will you do to get what you want? What will you do to take better care of yourself?

EXERCISE 4B – RELIANCE, ERODING

Ask only for what you truly need. The fourth rudimentary skill necessary to building healthy reliance is asking only for the help you truly need. Don't ask for something you can do for yourself. Do all that you can for yourself and, only then, ask for help. If you want a new job, polish your résumé, talk to recruiters, submit applications, and, only then, ask your friend to put in a good work for you at work. The people in your life will appreciate the effort you have expended to solve your own problems and will realize that you are asking for help that you need and for something you can't supply. This sets up a positive dynamic for the people who care about you. They will feel good about making a contribution that helps you.

TASK: Make a list of the things you need to do for yourself and those things that you need to ask of others. Review it every day this week and make sure you aren't asking for something that you can do for yourself.

SESSION 3

EXERCISE 1C – RELIANCE, ERODING

Show appreciation for help you receive. In order to be more successful at healthy reliance on others, you must be skilled at maintaining the productive relationships you have. If people become disheartened or discouraged by their efforts to assist you, they will quickly tire and give up. You will have to find a constant supply of new people, which may not be easy. Session 3 focuses your attention on how you can better maintain those kind people who care for you and want to be helpful.

Exercise 1 invites you to consider your skill at showing appreciation for the help you receive. Most people simply want to hear from you that you notice and value their efforts to support you. Many people are uncomfortable openly expressing appreciation.

TASK: We invite you to practice this week by openly appreciating someone at least three times each day. Make sure your appreciations are honest and clear.

EXERCISE 2C – RELIANCE, ERODING

Demonstrate that you are using assistance to make positive change. The second skill in maintaining a robust and useful support network is to demonstrate that the assistance you receive is making a difference. They are investing in your life and are hoping that, as a result of their investment, your life is getting better and stronger. If not, they may feel it is useless to try to assist you.

TASK: We invite you to take on the responsibility of using their assistance to its fullest benefit and then telling your network how you used their help and the result you created. Focus on one instance where others are supporting you now. How are you using their assistance? Now, how could you use it even more effectively? Write down your answers. Now, put your insights into practice.

EXERCISE 3C – RELIANCE, ERODING

Show that you can maintain forward momentum. The third critical skill in maintaining your support network is to show that you can continue to make forward momentum in making your life better. Not only do people want to see that they can be helpful, they want to know that you can sustain and expand the progress they have assisted you in making. If you get better in one area of your life and then fall down in some other area, your friends can become discouraged that you aren't using their assistance to get your act together.

TASK: Step back and take a comprehensive view of your life. Are there areas that are strong and some that are weak? Are you addressing the weak ones? Do you have bad habits that perpetually undermine the progress you make? Do you sabotage yourself when things go too well? These are common patterns people fall into. If you need assistance breaking free, please call one of our coaches.

EXERCISE 4C – RELIANCE, ERODING

Provide assistance to those who have assisted you. Even though your life is eroding, you are not without the ability to provide support and assistance to others. In fact, one of the ways you will stem your erosion and begin to strengthen your life is to shift from that which you need to that which you can provide. The easiest and most effective place to do that is with those who are supporting you.

TASK: Make a list of each person who is currently supporting you. Next to each name write something you can do to assist them. It could be as simple as watching their dog when they are out of town, taking a meal to them when they are sick, or calling to encourage them when they are in a tough spot. Begin to focus on doing something to support someone in your network each day.

SESSION 4

EXERCISE 1D – RELIANCE, ERODING

Network with people who have effective lives. Session 4 focuses on some issues that make your reliance on others sustainable. It is of little value to build a useful network only to have it fall into disrepair.

Exercise 1 invites you to build a valuable network. It is easy to populate your network with people who are just like you. You know what they say, "Birds of a feather flock together." But, in truth, birds of a feather are not very useful. You won't benefit much from filling your network with people whose lives are eroding. They are having their own issues and don't have many resources with which to help you. You would benefit much more from inviting into your network people who have their act together, who are moving forward in achieving their goals.

TASK: This week we invite you to make a list of the people you know who are either growing or thriving.

EXERCISE 2D – RELIANCE, ERODING

Inviting others into your network: Now that you have a list of people who would strengthen your network, you will need to develop the skills to invite them. It is likely that you haven't yet built a sufficiently strong relationship with them to simply extend an invitation. It will take time to cultivate the relationship until it is a natural step for them to think of themselves as part of your network. This process starts small.

TASK: Consider some way that you can begin speaking to this person. Perhaps you look for opportunities to greet them or to ask about their weekend. After a few weeks, you might invite them to coffee or lunch, during which you get to know more about their lives. After a month or so, you might invite them out to dinner and use the time to inquire as to ways you might support them. When the time is right, you should ask them if they will be part of your support network. Be prepared to share with them exactly what that means. Make it comfortable for them to decline or to accept.

EXERCISE 3D – RELIANCE, ERODING

Study their habits and disciplines and learn from them.

TASK: Now that you are upgrading the quality of your network, begin to pay attention to the habits and disciplines of those whose lives are in better shape than your own. One of the great benefits of having a strong network is that it puts you in proximity to people who have valuable lessons for you to learn. If one of your friends has done a better job cultivating her career than you have, ask her what she did. If someone has a more functional relationship with his teenagers than you do, inquire as to how he developed that kind of relationship with them. Lessons like this are free, and you will benefit greatly from the wisdom of your network.

EXERCISE 4D – RELIANCE, ERODING

Solve whatever issues have been causing your life to erode. The whole purpose of these exercises is to build the resources for you to build a stronger life for yourself. A robust network and healthy reliance on them are powerful tools, but tools are useful only if you put them to work.

TASK: We invite you to list the issues that are causing your life to erode. Now, prioritize it. Which is the most important issue to solve first? Often, one is necessary to solve before the others can be addressed. Now, what assistance do you need to resolve that issue? How can your network help you? Ask for help and get to work.

FACTOR – RELIANCE

The ability to gain, utilize, and maintain the support of others.

SELF-ASSESSED RATING - TREADING WATER

You have built a stable and useful network of people on whom you can rely when needed.

SESSION 1

EXERCISE 1A – RELIANCE, TREADING WATER

Check your network; are your friends treading water too? You are treading water in your life largely because you don't have a robust network of people on whom you can rely for assistance when needed. Session 1 is designed to assist you in better understanding your current network and how it is helping, and, perhaps, limiting a life in which you are fully thriving.

Exercise 1 invites you to consider who is in your network. You may have heard it said that your life is the summation of your five closest relationships. There is a lot of truth in the idea that your life isn't richer than that of the people with whom you most closely associate. A big part of healthy reliance is built on a network of people whose lives are in order and who are growing and thriving.

TASK: Get out a sheet of paper or your computer or tablet and write down your 10 closest friends. Think of the people on whom you rely for advice, support, and/or assistance. Now, next to each name evaluate their lives. Are they hanging on by their fingernails, eroding, treading water, growing, or thriving? If almost everyone in your network is treading water at best, you have some work to do.

EXERCISE 2A – RELIANCE, TREADING WATER

Are you using your friendships to justify coasting? One of the ways we can justify being stuck in our lives is to commiserate with others whose lives are as stuck as our own. In Exercise 2 we are inviting you to pay attention to how you and your closest friends and associates speak to one another. If you and your friends tend to complain about your lives and blame others or circumstances for the fact you aren't growing, you are reinforcing each other in treading water. On the other hand, if you are helping each other to solve problems and encouraging each other to persevere through changes, you are helping each other grow and thrive.

TASK: Over the next week, whenever you are with your friends, pay attention to the conversations they have with you and you have with them. At the end of each day, evaluate whether you are reinforcing each other in your "stuckness" or encouraging each other to grow. Begin to shape your conversations with your friends toward encouragement. Invite them to do the same.

EXERCISE 3A – RELIANCE, TREADING WATER

While noticing how you interact, do you reinforce each other for being stuck? One of the most valuable ways we benefit from reliance on others is to be encouraged to be changing those things that are limiting our lives and to be developing better habits. Research has proven the value of a support network for making constructive changes in our lives. You may intend to go to the gym every morning at 7:00, but if you have a training buddy who drops by your house each day at 6:45 to go to the gym with you, you are much more likely to stick with your commitment.

TASK: List the times you can recall when your network of friends and family encouraged you to stick with a healthy change or actually joined you in the commitment. Now, list all of the times when you did the same for those same people. We want you to invite your support network to join you in one change you want to make in your life now. See who will sign up to either take on that same challenge or to daily check in with you while you are changing.

EXERCISE 4A – RELIANCE, TREADING WATER

Giving up envy. Exercise 4 invites you to consider how much you and your network have fallen into the bad habit of envying those who have more than you or have life easier in some way. It is easy for you and your network to fall into playing the victim role in life. There are always people who have life easier than we do. When we become envious, we shift our attention from how we can make our lives better to live in resentment of those who have more. Whatever energy we could apply to making constructive change is wasted. When we, or others, play the victim role, we invite our friends to join in. Our network can become a club of resentment.

TASK: Write down all instances where you and your friends and family are envious of others. Practice shifting from envy to some positive plan for constructive change. How will you get for yourself that which you are envious of in others?

SESSION 2

EXERCISE 1B – RELIANCE, TREADING WATER

Forming relationships with people you admire. We now invite you to shift your focus from assessing your network to strengthening it. One of the best ways to build an effective network on which you can establish healthy reliance is to invite people into your network whose lives are in better shape than your own. People you admire are great people for you to get to know. People who have resources will be able to use some of their resources to assist you. People who know other people can use their network to open doors.

TASK: Make a list of all of the people you know who might be valuable to be in your network. Work on this list every day this week, adding names that come to mind.

EXERCISE 2B – RELIANCE, TREADING WATER

Take out your list from last week. These are people you want to invite into your support network. You may be able to directly ask some of these people into your circle because they know you well and would welcome the invitation to support you. Some people actually create an informal "board of directors" for their lives that is composed of influential and wise people who regularly give advice and support. For others, you will need to begin building relationships. That might include meeting for coffee or lunch, or having someone to your home for dinner. Extending yourself to build relationships is a critical skill in developing a robust support network.

TASK: Create a plan for inviting four new people into your network and begin putting it into play.

EXERCISE 3B – RELIANCE, TREADING WATER

Building win/win relationships. Now that you are building a more useful and valuable network, it is important for you to create a positive interpersonal dynamic within this group. People are far more open to support you if they feel that you are there to support them. Building win/win relationships helps to sustain the reciprocity that makes reliance work. Write down the names of everyone in your support network. Next to each name, write down a list of issues where that person needs assistance or support. Pick those issues where you have the ability to be of assistance.

TASK: Create an action plan for providing assistance and support to those people. Make sure your plan is reasonable and sustainable. Now, put it into play.

EXERCISE 4B – RELIANCE, TREADING WATER

Taking ownership for your ambition. It is of no value to have a rich and useful support network unless you have the drive to move forward to improve your life. In Exercise 4 we invite you to own your ambition. It is good to want things—especially those things that make your life more meaningful and valuable. The more accepting you are of your ambition and the clearer you are as to what you want, the more useful your network will be to you. The people who care for you want to support you, and they need to know how they can do that effectively.

TASK: Make a list of the things you want to achieve and to change. Now, next to each, write what others can do to help and support you. Give this some thought. Some of your contacts may have resources. Others will have contacts. Others will be able to challenge and support you. Write what you need and from whom. Now, ask each person if they will help.

SESSION 3

EXERCISE 1C – RELIANCE, TREADING WATER

Asking for help to open doors. One of the important ways reliance can be useful to you is in opening doors. You are certainly aware of how competitive life can be. You may want a new job but you will compete with hundreds of other applicants for that position. You may send in your résumé and never hear anything back. How do you distinguish yourself in order to secure the opportunity you seek? One of the most powerful tools to get yourself noticed is your support network. The people you know also know other people. They can open doors for you by asking their friends and colleagues to at least take a look at your application. That little bit of assistance can make a vast difference for you.

TASK: Make a list of advantages you have received because people opened doors for you. Now, list any doors you might need opened. Can any of your friends help? If not, do they know anyone who might be able to? Reach out to them and ask.

EXERCISE 2C – RELIANCE, TREADING WATER

Asking for help only when you need it. A second skill in building healthy self-reliance is to ask for only those things you truly need. Another way of stating this is that you should do all that you can to help yourself and ask for help only when you have exhausted all other avenues. People want to help you, but they also want to know that you *need* their help rather than just *want* it. You demonstrate that you need help when you try every way you know to solve your own problems.

TASK: Make a list of the assistance you have requested (or received) from your support network. Next to each item, note anywhere you could have done more to solve your own problems. Do you have more of those or more of the items where you exhausted all of your resources? We want you to work on making sure that you never ask for help until you actually need it.

EXERCISE 3C – RELIANCE, TREADING WATER

Asking for specific things. A third skill in building healthy reliance on others is to be specific in your requests of others. It isn't helpful to your friends when you bring them a big problem to solve. Instead, they would like to know what is the one clear and specific thing you need. You might need one introduction. Or, you might need someone to watch your dog for one hour. Or, you might need a ride on Tuesday to a job interview. Practice becoming very clear about the one thing that you need and then asking your support network to help you by providing it or helping you to secure it.

TASK: Take one issue where you want to move ahead in your life and see if you can determine the one thing you most need that you can't do for yourself. Write it down. Who in your network might be able to help? Ask them this week.

EXERCISE 4C – RELIANCE, TREADING WATER

Showing appreciation for assistance. Finally, practice showing appreciation to those who have assisted you. The people who help you are extending themselves. They have no obligation to go out of their way to assist you. Often, the only reward they want is to know that their help mattered to you. Sometimes people are reluctant to openly express appreciation because it feels like a weakness or they are uncomfortable being so vulnerable. But, the skill of expressing appreciation is very useful in reinforcing the support you are seeking from others and in sustaining the care others have for you. The format for effective appreciation is simple. Speak to the person face-to-face if possible. Thank them for their assistance and name exactly what they did for you. Tell them how it was helpful to you.

TASK: Make a list of people to whom you could express some appreciation and practice showing appreciation to one person each day for the next week.

SESSION 4

EXERCISE 1D – RELIANCE, TREADING WATER

Using assistance to its fullest. Session 4 will invite you to focus on skills that help you sustain healthy reliance on others. There are several skills that encourage people to continue to support you and several that will prevent people from burning out in their desire to assist you. The first, and perhaps most important, is to demonstrate that you are using the assistance you requested to actually create forward momentum in your life. The fact that you have been treading water is obvious not only to you but to those who care about you as well. They want to see that you have gotten yourself unstuck and are actually growing. If you don't demonstrate substantial and positive change, your friends will grow resistant to requests for aid in the future.

TASK: Take a few moments to assess the critical issues you need to address in order to demonstrate the change everyone wants you to make. Are you ready to change? If not, don't ask for help until you are. When you are, ask for assistance and change.

EXERCISE 2D – RELIANCE, TREADING WATER

Reciprocity. A second skill that helps you to sustain the health and vitality of your reliance on others is reciprocity. While we have asked you to focus on your needs and how to extract support in a constructive way, we now invite you to consider the needs of those in your support network. What resources do you have that can benefit your friends in their quest to build a better life? Often, we become so focused on our needs that we overlook the skills, contacts, and opportunities we have available. Take some time to list all of the resources you have that you could use to help your friends.

TASK: List the names of the people in your support network. Write down any needs they have with which you might be able to assist. Find time this week to offer your help to each person.

EXERCISE 3D – RELIANCE, TREADING WATER

Continuing to expand your network. Your support network is dynamic. People will drop out because they move away, become interested in other things, or the relationship simply grows apart. Those things happen. You should always be on the lookout for new members to add to this group. Keep in mind that as your life gets stronger, you should look for people who are better equipped to help you on your journey. In other words, you should always be upgrading your support network.

TASK: Start a list of people who might be good candidates to add to your list in the future. Revisit this list every month to add new names. Begin building these relationships as we outlined in earlier exercises because it takes time to cultivate a new member of your network.

EXERCISE 4D – RELIANCE, TREADING WATER

Using your network to assist others. Finally, your network has application beyond your needs and the needs of those in your network. Caring for the needs of others is a wonderful way for you to expand your life and to enrich the lives of those in your network. Everyone benefits from knowing that they are making a positive difference in the world. Supporting a cause gives meaning and purpose to our lives. There are always abundant opportunities for us to rally our network and to contribute our own resources to address the needs in our local community. Needs such as feeding the poor, caring for the homeless, community cleanup projects, etc. are powerful ways to open our eyes and the eyes of others to the value they have to offer others.

TASK: Make a list of some causes that interest you and consider how you can bring them to the attention of your network.

FACTOR – RELIANCE

The ability to gain, utilize, and maintain the support of others.

SELF-ASSESSED RATING - GROWING

You have earned the support of people who not only believe in you but have substantial resources to support you when needed.

SESSION 1

EXERCISE 1A – RELIANCE, GROWING

Robust support network. Is it lopsided or missing any important resources? The fact that you are growing speaks well to your ability to rely on others for assistance and support. However, you may have some fine-tuning to do in order to optimize your support network.

TASK: Please list everyone you consider to be part of your network—those people on whom you can rely. Now, answer the following questions: 1. Is my network too focused on people who are like me? 2. Does my network sufficiently include people of greater success and resources than mine? 3. Is my network adequately diverse? 4. Is my network lopsided in any way? 5. Does my network lack any important resource that I might need? Your answers to these questions can guide you in adding new members to your support group to make it even more useful.

EXERCISE 2A – RELIANCE, GROWING

Being aware of how you are known by your network. Your friends have a way of viewing you. It is who you have become in their thinking. They see you as competent, needy, stuck, leading, complaining, or in some other way. This is how you have made yourself known to them, and it matters because they will tend to relate to you according to how they view you. If they see you as a needy person, they will tend to overlook your efforts to be more independent. If they see you as a complainer, they will encourage you to complain. It can be difficult to build a healthier pattern of reliance unless we first build a healthy way of being known by the people who know us best.

TASK: Over the next week, pay attention to how your network of friends relates to you and see if you can determine how they view you. If you are able, summarize it in one or two words. Then, reflect on the impact of how you are currently being viewed. Does it invite the support you want? Will it help you build a better life? If not, you will need to decide on a better way to be viewed by your friends and then to show up with them in that new way. Over time, it will change how they view you and relate to you.

EXERCISE 3A – RELIANCE, GROWING

Optimizing how you are known by your network. Many people are unaware of how they are known by those around them. Even fewer know that they can decide how they want to be known. It is as easy as changing our story about the world and who we choose to be in it. Everyone has a "story" about life. That story sets our expectations for what we want from our lives and how we show up in it. If I think the world is welcoming and kind, I will show up open. If, on the other hand, I think the world is dangerous, I will show up defensive and protective. We can change that story whenever we choose.

TASK: Write down your story about life and who you are in the context of that story. Now you know why you are showing up as you are. Do you like how you are being? Can you think of a better way to be?

EXERCISE 4A – RELIANCE, GROWING

Changing your story. Last week you identified your story about life that shapes who you are being. Remember, it is just a story. That being the case, you can create a new story whenever you choose. If your story was that life is hard, you could change it to life being easy. If your story was that everyone must struggle to get ahead, you could change it to life will give you whatever you want. The great thing about changing your story is that you get to be different because of your new story.

TASK: Write a new story about life. It doesn't have to be true. It is only a story. Now, decide how you want to be based on your new story. Write it down. Now, practice being that person every day. You will be amazed at how differently people will perceive you.

SESSION 2

EXERCISE 1B – RELIANCE, GROWING

Keeping in touch with your network. Keeping your support network healthy and responsive takes attention and some work. In Session 2 we will share some skills that you might use to keep your network responsive. First, get to know details about the people in your network, especially those things that are important to them. You should know the name of their spouse, their children's names and ages, their hobbies and interests, where they work, and what they do. All of this information allows you to build closer relationships, ones that become friendships that can last a lifetime.

TASK: Write down the names of the people in your network and what you know and don't know about them. Begin filling in the gaps and keeping that information someplace where you can update it as things change.

EXERCISE 2B – RELIANCE, GROWING

The second tool in keeping your network strong is to celebrate milestones in their lives. Make it a point to send birthday and anniversary cards. Congratulate them on their work anniversary and on things like their children's school graduations. By celebrating successes and special events, you remind your friends that they are special to you and that you take the time to pay attention to them. When we give people loving attention, it is often returned. By paying attention to others, they will pay more attention to you. Social media platforms like Facebook and LinkedIn will remind you of some of the special events in the lives of your network. You should also share special events in your life and the life of your family. Sharing invites greater intimacy and care.

TASK: Start sharing and paying attention. Make a list of upcoming events you can make special for someone else.

EXERCISE 3B – RELIANCE, GROWING

The third tool is to keep in regular touch with your network. Send news articles or anything you read that is relevant to your friends. If you have someone in your network who loves fishing, send them fishing stories from time to time. Send notes of encouragement or just to say you were thinking of them. Use commuting time to call the people in your network. You don't have to have a reason to call other than to simply check in. Even if you leave a voicemail message, you are communicating that you care and are bringing your relationship front of mind. You should consider touching base in some way each week with everyone in your network.

TASK: Make a plan as to how you will do this over the next week.

EXERCISE 4B – RELIANCE, GROWING

A fourth tool to strengthen your network is to use it to create an informal board of directors for your life and your work. The idea of a board of directors is to recruit people of experience, talent, and capability who can oversee and advise a business. Not only is such a group useful for a business, it can be extremely beneficial for your life project. Be very careful to pick the most competent and capable people you know. If possible, select them for the skills and experience you need to move forward in your life.

TASK: Set up regular times to meet. These might be four to six times each year. Make sure each meeting has an agenda of issues you want to discuss that is distributed well in advance of the meeting. Ask for input on those issues and construct an action plan based on their input. Report back to each member on the progress you have made.

SESSION 3

EXERCISE 1C – RELIANCE, GROWING

In Session 3 we invite you to fine tune how you interact with your network to optimize your reliance on them. In Exercise 1 we ask you to consider your willingness to be candid. The people who care about you can assist you only to the extent they understand the issues you are facing. It might seem natural to keep your challenges to yourself lest you expose your weaknesses and neediness to others. But doing so limits the value of your network to assist you. We want you to become comfortable sharing everything that is relevant with your network.

TASK: Make a list of all relevant issues that you are withholding from the people on whom you rely. Next to each, write down why you are holding back and what you stand to gain and to lose by sharing the information. Now, take the least threatening topic on your list and share it. Work your way through the entire list.

EXERCISE 2C – RELIANCE, GROWING

Now, we invite you to consider how open you are to receive honest and constructive feedback from your network. In order for people to really support you, they need to know that you want their input and won't become angry or defensive regardless of what they tell you. While they might not always be right in the advice they give, they are assisting you because they care about you. Their feedback is always well-intentioned. Often when we resist feedback and advice it is because we know there is some truth in it that we don't want to face. You must get beyond such reactions to optimize your reliance.

TASK: Make a list of feedback you have resisted or are resisting. Apologize to the person you resisted and invite them to give you that feedback again. Seek to learn and to change from the lessons you learn.

EXERCISE 3C – RELIANCE, GROWING

Exercise 3 invites you to focus on the extent to which you put the support and assistance of your network to use. The people who care for you and try to help you want to know that you actually utilize the care they provide. You can best show this to them by turning their assistance into clear and written action plans that you disseminate with your network. Your action plans should include the issue that you brought up, the advice or support that was given, and what you plan to do to put that support to work to strengthen your life. Include dates when you will have completed each step. By sharing these plans, your network will know that you take their involvement in your life seriously and intend to use their resources and support wisely.

TASK: Take time now to write two or three action plans for support your network has recently given to you. Share those plans.

EXERCISE 4C – RELIANCE, GROWING

Exercise 4 invites you to become more focused on sharing with your network the outcome of your action plans. It is one thing to take advice and to use it. It is another thing to share with others precisely how following their advice or using their support actually helped you. It is those positive advances in your life that are most encouraging to the people who care about you. They want to see you build an even more effective life.

TASK: You should keep a running list of the outcomes of the issues you are addressing and update that list regularly. You should send out periodic updates to your network sharing the successes (and failures) of the things you have tried. People will greatly appreciate your keeping them informed about your progress. Take time now to list some outcomes and then share those with your network.

SESSION 4

EXERCISE 1D – RELIANCE, GROWING

Session 4 will address larger issues that are designed to expand your awareness of allowing your reliance on others to blossom into something bigger than your needs.

Exercise 1 focuses on cultivating a spirit of appreciation. The people who support you are gifts to you. You don't deserve their care and help. They are willing to help you without pay or reward of any kind. They do so from the kindness of their hearts. It is so important that you pay attention to the grace and goodness they extend toward you and that you allow it to fill you with gratitude. As you expand your ability to notice and value that goodness, learn to express it to your network in open appreciation.

TASK: Regularly tell each person how much you value them and appreciate them for their assistance. Make this part of your ongoing communication with each of them.

EXERCISE 2D – RELIANCE, GROWING

Make reliance on others a two-way street. Your network has gifts and abilities that are useful to you, and you have gifts and abilities that are useful to them. Begin asking them about the issues in their lives and sharing your resources, advice, and guidance with them whenever you can. You have the ability to make your reliance a mutual relationship of helping each other rather than a one-sided relationship where you are always the object of assistance. Mutual relationships are much easier to sustain and are more durable.

TASK: Make a list of the needs of your network. Reach out to them this week and ask them how you can be of assistance.

EXERCISE 3D – RELIANCE, GROWING

Exercise 3 invites you to extend your ability to be helpful beyond your network. Who do you know to whom you can be a source of guidance or assistance? Offering yourself as a resource to others shifts your focus from your needs to your abundance. It seems that whatever you give to life, life will give back to you. Hence, if you abundantly give your assistance to others, the world will assist you even more. This is a powerful principle to put into play in your life. Doing so also allows you to see more clearly all that you have and all that you have accomplished. You see yourself as strong and resourceful rather than needy. You carry yourself with more power and dignity.

TASK: Make a list of five people you know who might benefit from your support. Approach them this week to inquire if they want your support.

EXERCISE 4D – RELIANCE, GROWING

Exercise 4 invites you to use your network and those whom you are supporting to take on a cause bigger than yourself. Everyone needs meaning and purpose in their lives. As people expand their purpose, their lives take on a bigger and richer perspective. You can invite the people around you to take on some project that will make a difference in their community. There is an abundance of such projects if we open our eyes to them. It could be a neighborhood watch, community cleanup, taking meals to shut-ins, feeding the homeless, or helping to build homes in the inner city. Projects of this sort build a mutual reliance that extends beyond our personal needs to care for the needs of the world.

TASK: Make a list of projects you could consider addressing. Pick one and recruit your network and the people you know to help. Be the leader and organizer of this project.

Made in the USA
Middletown, DE
18 January 2018